REMEDIAL

LESSONS
AT A MOMENT'S NOTICE

REMEDIAL

LESSONS
AT A MOMENT'S NOTICE

by Chris Lakey B. Phil., M. Ed.

W. FOULSHAM & CO. LIMITED
LONDON · NEW YORK · TORONTO · CAPE TOWN · SYDNEY

W. Foulsham & Co. Limited
Yeovil Road, Slough, Berks., England

ISBN 0-572-01412-0

Printed in Great Britain by
Hazell Watson & Viney Limited,
Aylesbury, Bucks

Acknowledgements

I would like to thank my wife, Cherrie, for her help and tolerance, to Neil Green of PBS for micro and print-out facilities, and many other practising teachers with whom I have discussed the contents of this book.

Contents

Introduction

The lessons in this book are intended to help teachers who may, at short notice, have to teach groups of pupils who for one reason or another have deficiencies in their basic literacy and numeracy skills. This will include low achievers in mainstream schools (often referred to as the 'remedial' pupils), as well as pupils who are classified formally as having 'special educational needs', and who may be receiving their education in a special school environment. Teaching in this context is an extremely difficult undertaking, and this book hopes to make the task a little easier.

It is intended that each lesson is an entity, though some suggestions are made for follow-up work. Unless it is otherwise indicated the only requirements for each lesson are board and chalk for the teacher, and pencil and paper for the pupils.

My own experience working with low achievers suggests that generally they do not enjoy the written word, since it comes to them only with difficulty, if at all. Therefore many of the lessons in the book involve little or no writing, and often only a limited amount of reading. The main content of many sessions is language based, since this overcomes to some extent the teacher needing to know the literacy and numeracy abilities of the pupils involved. This immediately removes one potential problem area.

It follows logically from this that if the pupils are not primarily engaged in reading and writing activities, then they must be actively engaged in something else for the lessons to be successful. This something else is thought and discussion, along with group work and individual activity (learning through doing). It is important with the less able or under-achieving pupil to keep the learning interesting, and it is for that reason that many of the lessons are in the form of games. This can provide stimulation whilst also reinforcing basic educational concepts.

Similarly it is argued, and research seems to verify this, that many 'remedial' pupils (or those with 'special educational needs') are taught their basic English and Maths separately, but they are included in mixed ability groups for many of the other curricular activities. It is less likely that another teacher will be expected to take the 'remedials' for a lesson such as art, home economics, media studies or even history, geography or science. Nevertheless, I have presumed that such an occasion might occur and have included a limited number of such sessions in traditionally 'specialist' subjects.

The outline has been divided into sections for convenience. Sections 1–3 offer lessons in the basic skills, and Sections 4–6 offer some lessons in particular 'subject' areas. In the index there is an indication of the content of each lesson. Teaching objectives are also clearly stated for each lesson.

The layout of the lessons is simple and in a prescriptive format. However, circumstances will vary enormously and the implementation of each lesson is entirely dependent on the interpretation of the individual teacher. The lesson 'plans' are starting points or guidelines, and it is important to be prepared to respond to the needs of a particular group of pupils. This can vary according to the age and ability of the class, and variations of the lesson plans are offered to take account of this.

1

Improving Spelling (Basic English)

WORD SEARCH

The objective of this lesson is to encourage the pupils to look for frequently occurring groups of letters which might constitute one of the nominated words in the word search.

1. The word search grid can either be photocopied or written up on to the board. (The publisher gives permission to photocopy the grid)

2. Explain to the pupils that the wordsearch contains the names of towns and cities in Britain. Their task is to find these and write them out.

3. The towns and cities are Birmingham, Manchester, Glasgow, London, Newcastle, Belfast, Cardiff, Southampton, Bristol, Norwich, Reading, Maidenhead, Leeds, Portsmouth, Liverpool, Aberdeen, Sheffield, Coventry, Derby, Bath.

4. In addition the pupils are also to make a second list of other words which they can find in the grid. These need to be circled on their page.if an accurate check is to be kept of correct answers.

5. There is no definitive list for this second level activity, since any English word that is to be found in the dictionary is acceptable.

6. In many cases words will be found as constituent parts of the longer place names e.g. Nottingham contains in, am, not, tin, ham, no.

7. Words can only be found from strings of consecutive letters either horizontally, vertically or diagonally in any direction.

8. If pupils find difficulty in locating the original list of place names, they can either be given initial letters, or even the full name.

9. An extension activity may be to take one place name such as Manchester, and use its letters in any order to make as many words as possible.

C	A	N	O	R	W	I	C	H	F	O	R	T	L	I
O	D	E	R	B	Y	B	O	Y	O	P	E	R	I	L
D	E	W	B	I	R	M	I	N	G	H	A	M	V	L
E	N	C	I	S	P	I	L	L	E	N	D	A	E	H
S	E	A	B	E	L	F	A	S	T	H	I	N	R	T
O	T	S	E	L	L	S	M	O	S	T	N	C	P	U
U	O	T	T	L	G	B	A	T	H	O	G	H	O	O
T	O	L	D	O	B	R	I	S	T	O	L	E	O	M
H	O	E	W	N	R	O	D	E	P	A	S	S	L	S
A	R	M	Y	D	A	L	E	E	D	S	I	T	O	T
M	I	A	C	O	V	E	N	T	R	Y	L	E	A	R
P	P	S	O	N	E	C	H	I	N	O	L	R	R	O
T	S	H	E	F	F	I	E	L	D	U	Y	E	S	P
O	P	E	N	T	W	O	A	B	E	R	D	E	E	N
N	E	S	T	C	A	R	D	I	F	F	I	D	E	A

HANGMAN

The objectives of this activity are to make the pupils aware of the most frequently used letters in the alphabet and to generally improve their spelling ability.

1. Begin by explaining how the game is played.
2. The salient points are
   a. The number of spaces indicate the number of letters
   b. Each correct guess fills in the appropriate space
   c. Each incorrect guess concedes one element of the 'gallows'
   d. A guess can be made at an incomplete word, but if incorrect this also is penalised as in c.
   e. The completed 'hung-man' is victory for the questionner
   f. The completed word is victory for the respondent
   g. There are 11 elements in the completed 'hung-man'

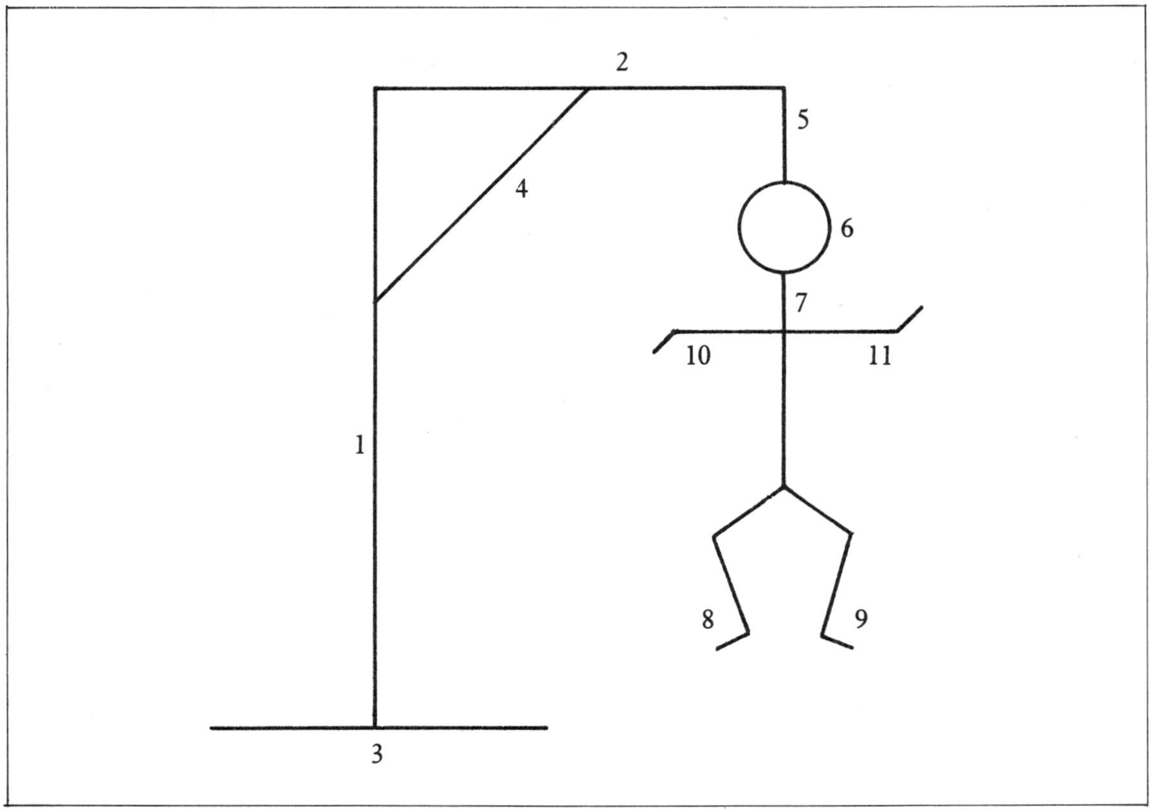

3. If pupils are unfamiliar with the game draw the hangman.

4. Write up the requisite number of blank spaces on the board for a demonstration game. If necessary the alphabet can also be written above and letters crossed off when used.

5. Class members take turns in guessing a letter until either the word is finished or guessed, or the hangman figure is complete. Words (or phrases) can be used dependent on the age/ability of the class group.
Some suggestions are given below:-

1	2	3
open	unlucky	handkerchief
number	right	defended
house	mistake	carefully
school	aeroplane	station
chair	elephant	permission
Monday	robot	entangled

6. The class can be divided into teams to extend the activity. The teams can take it in turns to answer teacher devised problems or play against each other using pencil and paper. Alternatively the class can be divided into pairs.

7. In these latter pupil-centred activities the criterion is that the questioner (or team) know the correct spelling of the word, and give the correct information on questioning. It may be wise to encourage pupils to keep note of their guesses to avoid disagreements. The teacher may also wish to check any spellings before they are used in the game.

8. Points can be awarded for getting the correct answer, being able to read it, setting correct spellings, and 'hanging' the opponent. The winning team or individual is decided by who has the most points.

9. It may be that the pupils might enjoy a theme for the game such as pop groups or TV programmes. These may consist of several words.

ANAGRAMS

The objectives of this activity are to improve spelling by looking 'into' words, and additionally to look for contextual clues, in this case classifications.

1. The activity can be either on an individual basis or in small groups introducing an element of competition. There is a theme to each set of words, which may or may not be given to the pupils in advance by way of providing a clue.

2. Each of the lists below are in ascending order of difficulty and complexity. They can either be offered in full with a class of widely varying abilities, or alternatively split into easier and harder sections. If required less able or younger pupils can be given the initial letter of each word used.

3. The teacher writes the jumbled word onto the board. The pupils must unscramble the words and rewrite them with the correct spelling.

4. For pupils with very limited literacy abilities it may be necessary to provide lists of anagrams with only a few letters such as three or four to provide success in the first instance.

Sports		**Clothes**	
loop	polo	aht	hat
logf	golf	octa	coat
nnsite	tennis	sskoc	socks
guryb	rugby	voelgs	gloves
onkorse	snooker	hesos	shoes
mgmiinws	swimming	akorna	anorak
lolboatf	football	tgsith	tights
atthcseli	athletics	ornaatic	raincoat
gniksta	skating	essotrur	trousers

Furniture

ebd	bed
hacir	chair
kins	sink
balet	table
roocke	cooker
oafs	sofa
losto	stool
oniap	piano
braupcod	cupboard
brodwera	wardrobe
gerrofetarri	refrigerator

Domestic Animals

tca	cat
god	dog
osume	mouse
bitabr	rabbit
rroatp	parrot
stermah	hamster
lodfghis	goldfish
bilger	gerbil
gehohged	hedgehog
nugiae gip	guinea pig
eggarrubid	budgerigar

Occupations

tocdor	doctor
refmar	farmer
runse	nurse
sittden	dentist
chareet	teacher
mistech	chemist
remainf	fireman
canepilom	policeman
kersheepop	shopkeeper

Transport

sub	bus
pish	ship
axit	taxi
panel	plane
hocac	coach
roylr	lorry
koomibert	motorbike
bulamcane	ambulance
cripolhete	helicopter

A–Z INITIAL LETTER GAME

The objective of this lesson is to encourage pupils to associate letter sounds with words. This activity is a whole class game and is teacher-centred.

1. Group the pupils in a semi-circle around the board.

2. Write up the alphabet if this is required for that particular group (though if this is necessary a few minutes preliminary 'drill' practice repeating the alphabet would not go amiss!).

3. Teacher suggests the starting point
   a. 'I went to the supermarket and I bought. . . .'
   b. 'I went to the zoo and I saw a. . . .'
   c. 'I went for a ride on a bus/train and I saw a. . . .'
   d. 'I have a (male/female) friend whose name is. . . .'
   e. Any other one line which may take the interest of the particular group eg. pop stars, place names, types of car etc.

4. Each pupil will take a turn using successive letters of the alphabet and keeping to the theme.

5. Write the words on the board as they are offered.

6. Successive pupils then have to read the full list before adding their own contribution with the next initial letter.

7. Difficult letters eg. q, x, z can be omitted if it is felt appropriate.

8. Variations for older or more able pupils might involve
   a. Using the same activity, but using auditory memory instead of writing the list on the board.
   b. Compiling their own written lists either individually or in small groups (praise originality of thought and accuracy of spelling).
   c. The chosen letter can be somewhere other than at the beginning of the word. This will help word analysis skills.
   d. The pupils can write their own suggestions up on the board in the original game format.

ALPHABETICAL ORDER

The objective of this lesson is to practice alphabetical sequencing.

1. The first thing to ascertain is whether or not the pupils know the alphabet. If some do not then it is necessary to write it up on the board — this does not diminish the value of the exercise, but it is important to stress that it should be learnt by heart.

2. There are many practical instances in which a knowledge of the alphabet, and more especially of alphabetical order, are essential. Ask the pupils if they can think of any examples. Some of the more obvious ones are telephone directories, dictionaries, address books, street maps, and a whole variety of indexes.

3. Often information needs to be sought by consulting alphabetical lists so it is vital to learn the alphabet and acquire the skill of locating a particular entry through its spelling. Before this stage is reached the pupil needs to understand the principles behind alphabetic sequencing. The graded lists provided below will allow pupils to practice this skill from a simple to a more complex level, and permit them to work at their own rate.

4. It should also be pointed out that it is not necessary to be able to read all of the words in order to sequence them correctly. The pupils should be asked to begin with the first list and work progressively through. The lists can be shortened for younger pupils or those of very low ability by removing some of the words (remember of course that this will invalidate the answers depending on which words are removed).

List 1	**Answer**	**List 2**	**Answer**
back	arm	house	barn
leg	back	church	church
neck	foot	school	garage
arm	hand	pub	house
hand	leg	garage	pub
foot	neck	barn	school

List 3	Answer	List 4	Answer
car	bike	cabbage	apple
van	bus	peas	banana
bus	car	beetroot	beetroot
train	ship	apple	cabbage
ship	taxi	plum	orange
bike	train	banana	peas
taxi	van	orange	plum

List 5	Answer	List 6	Answer
monkey	elephant	ball	ball
elephant	emu	bunch	band
mouse	lion	bend	bath
lion	lizard	boat	bend
emu	llama	best	best
mongoose	mongoose	bath	boat
lizard	monkey	bread	bread
llama	mouse	band	bunch

List 7	Answer	List 8	Answer
coat	candle	drum	drag
cloak	card	drug	drain
cycle	cart	drumming	drink
clever	church	drop	drinking
cart	clever	drink	drop
candle	cloak	drag	drug
church	coach	drinking	drum
card	coat	drain	drumbeat
cutting	cutting	drummer	drummer
coach	cycle	drumbeat	drumming

5. This activity can be extended if necessary by asking any pupils who have completed their work to make a list similar to List 8 using a different consonant blend eg. cl, gr, str etc., or alternatively to put the names of the class in alphabetical order.

BASIC ENGLISH EXERCISES

The objective of this group of activities is to improve basic English and literacy skills.

This is not one lesson, but rather a variety of suggestions comprising some of the most frequently used approaches for teaching basic English. It can be adapted with relative ease to the circumstances of the particular class group.

The activities involved are comprehension, punctuation, dictation and cloze exercises. The level of each activity is entirely dependent on the age and ability of the class group.

A. Comprehension

1. Find a passage of suitable simplicity or complexity in a book; one of the pupils' regular workbooks would be appropriate.

2. Read out the passage, twice if necessary.

3. Ask the pupils questions which have answers explicit or implicit in the text. They are to write these down.

4. Offer some help with spelling if this is the problem since the activity is to test the understanding of the text.

B. Punctuation

1. Find a passage in a book which is within the ability of the class to read and understand.

2. Write the passage on to the board removing all punctuation and capital letters in doing so.

3. Read out the passage from the original text to give the pupils an awareness of its meaning when punctuated.

4. Explain if necessary that punctuation reflects speech patterns, and that if one stops to draw breath that is (or should be) a sentence end and requires a full stop. A pause in speech is represented by a comma, and that all new sentences and proper names begin with a capital letter.

C. Dictation

1. Once again it is necessary to find a passage of suitable simplicity or complexity for the specific group.

2. If necessary a string of related sentences can be made up, perhaps even to practice a particular word family or letter combination e.g. words with -igh(t).

3. Read out each sentence in full, then break the sentence down either into individual words or small phrases.

4. The pupils are to copy down the dictation, and may wish to mark each other's when the correct version is written up on the board at the end.

5. Simple primer readers have a controlled vocabulary and are useful for this activity if available.

D. Cloze

1. Here again it is necessary to select a suitable passage to suit the age and ability of the pupils.

2. The passage can either be read aloud leaving gaps which the pupils have to fill in, or alternatively written on the board with blank spaces indicating missing words.

3. Pupils are to fill in the missing words. The spelling is not critical because this activity promotes reading for meaning.

2

Using Language (Communication Skills)

DEFINITIONS/DESCRIPTIONS

The objectives for this activity are to improve expression and comprehension.

1. The class is divided into small groups or teams of three to five pupils.

2. One member of each small group is given a list of words.

3. This person has to describe or define the word to the rest of the group who try to guess the word.

4. The team are awarded one point for each correct answer.

5. Each group are allowed two minutes in which to guess as many words as possible in this way — one point for each correct guess.

6. Each group takes its turn consecutively.

7. The teacher's decision is final — no points are awarded if the word itself or a close derivation is used in the clue.

8. After each team has had their turn a different member of the first team has to define another list of words.

9. Begin by offering an example e.g. 'It is round' — 'A record'; 'It is yellow and round' — 'A ball'; 'It is yellow and round and hot, and shines in the sky' — 'The sun'.

10. The words below are in ascending order of difficulty depending on the age and ability level of the pupils involved. Lists A–D are parallel, as are lists E–H.

List A	List B	List C	List D
tree	flower	apple	banana
car	bus	plane	table
horse	dog	fish	boat
orange	jam	blue	chair
boy	girl	man	woman
yellow	green	red	blue
square	circle	triangle	oval
milk	beer	carrot	camel
bench	sink	settee	bed
lion	pond	stairs	circus
fair	house	flat	train
tram	town	branch	bucket
windmill	empty	push	carry
picture	hotel	trio	equal
football	happy	second	away

List E	List F	List G	List H
sprint	couple	elastic	juggle
Easter	sadness	family	cliff
daughter	seashore	private	untidy
rugby	surround	escape	different
bicycle	cupboard	telephone	student
workshop	cassette	handkerchief	chemist
underwear	garage	wardrobe	jaguar
anchor	carnival	earthquake	complete
produce	rectangle	overturn	excess
angry	refuse	contract	microphone

CONSEQUENTIAL THINKING

The objective of this lesson is to encourage the pupils to think laterally in problem-solving situations.

1. Divide the class into small discussion groups.

2. Set the scene with the following description 'You are the crew of a hot-air balloon which is losing height over shark infested water. The nearest land consists of two islands — one to the east is inhabited by cannibals with canoes and spears, and the other to the west is uninhabited, but has palm trees and a large population of rabbits. At present you are heading towards this island, but the wind may change and take you to the other one. The basket of the balloon is very full with various items. You will have to decide which ones to throw out to prevent losing more height. Arrange the following items in the order in which you would chose to throw them out.'

3. The contents of the basket are

   a. a coil of heavy rope
   b. first aid kit
   c. spare gas canister
   d. large can of fresh water
   e. hunting knife
   f. case of tinned food
   g. basket of fresh fruit
   h. 2 way radio
   i. binoculars
   j. inflatable lifeboat
   k. a book on 'survival'
   l. sandbags
   m. emergency kit (matches, compass, map, can opener)

   (this list to be written on the board)

4. The groups are now to make their choice for jettisoning the items. Each decision should be democratic and if possible unanimous before being recorded.

5. After completion of the list each group should write up their list, giving reasons verbally for their particular priority order.

6. If time allows a class group discussion can follow on the pros and cons of jettisoning certain of the items.

7. The task can be made easier by specifying only one of the islands as a destination. On the other hand it can be made harder by introducing other options, or even having the balloon change directions or other circumstances change during the course of the groups' deliberations.

8. There are no right and wrong answers, but credit can be given for sound logical thinking in this problem-solving activity.

EVENT SEQUENCING

The objectives for this activity are to encourage temporal sequencing and logical thought processes.

1. Explain to the pupils that certain activities follow particular sequences.

2. Give an example such as making a cup of tea. Talk this through highlighting the fact that later actions in the sequence are dependent on the earlier actions having been undertaken e.g. you cannot boil the kettle if the water has not been put in first, the tea will not be acceptable if the water has not been fully boiled or the tea (bag) is not in the pot.

3. Ask the pupils to set the following activity in the correct sequence. They can work in pairs or small groups if necessary.

   a. place the dishes on to the draining board
   b. pour hot water on to the dishes, cool water if needed
   c. put the dirty dishes in the washing-up bowl
   d. put the dishes away in the cupboard
   e. wash up the dishes one at a time
   f. pour in the washing-up liquid
   g. dry the dishes one at a time

4. The pupils may wish to insert their own stages dependent on the routine that they know, but stress that sometimes sequences may vary e.g. washing the crockery first, cutlery second and pans third may be their routine but not someone else's.

5. If the pupils are still unsure a second similar example can be used, but if they have succeeded in the sequencing they can now begin to formulate event sequences of their own. These can be written down or even represented diagrammatically.

6. Pupils should be encouraged to think of their own activities to analyse into temporal sequence, but a few suggestions include replacing a fuse, sewing on a button, putting petrol into a car at a self-service garage, using a launderette/doing the laundry at home, driving a car etc.

7. For younger or less able pupils the sequence may need to be more immediately relevant to their domestic routine e.g. brushing teeth, getting dressed, having a wash, coming to school etc.

CATEGORISATION

The main objective of this lesson is classification into categories dependent on certain criteria.

1. The pupils are asked to imagine that they are in a small town where there is no supermarket. There are only a selection of small shops which specialise in certain items.

2. The shops in this particular town are chemist, butcher, newsagent, grocer, hardware, greengrocer, clothes shop, electrical goods, and sports shop (these can be written on to the board). Other types of shops can be discussed with arguments for the need for a particular type of shop in a small town or village.

3. The class is divided into three groups which are given the following lists and asked to identify which of the shops in the imaginary town would provide the articles on their list.

List 1	**List 2**	**List 3**
notepad	onions	aspirin
batteries	sausages	tomatoes
mince	scarf	tennis ball
bandage	spaghetti	hammer
football	cassette recorder	shirt
nails	darts	magazine
sugar	potatoes	radio
suntan cream	plasters	chicken
apples	cigarettes	eggs
baked beans	beefburgers	pencil
skirt	padlock	cabbage

4. After successfully completing their own list the groups can exchange lists until they have completed all three.

5. Older or more able pupils with better reading ability and comprehension may progress to the following list also.

List 4	**List 5**	**List 6**
prescription	envelopes	mustard
twine	gloves	steak
chest freezer	paracetamol	courgette
veal	fan heater	cravatte
cooking oil	custard	gauze
periodicals	mandarin oranges	cigarette lighter
garlic	trowel	wallpaper paste
cardigan	turkey	squash racquet
shuttlecock	sweatband	video recorder

6. Pupils should then extend the list with items of their own choosing. This can be competitive with points awarded to the different teams for the number of items, originality of thought (e.g. aubergine is more unusual than peas or carrots), and correct spelling.

20 QUESTIONS

The objectives of this lesson are to encourage logical thought processes and promote a more precise use of language to elicit information.

1. Divide the class into two groups (teams), if possible of roughly equivalent ability.

2. Explain that the object of the game is to locate the answer solely through the use of questions which have a yes/no response.

3. Explain that the only clue to be given is animal, vegetable or mineral, and if necessary briefly explain what each of these might encompass.

4. Offer the pupils a few examples of the types of questions that they might ask initially e.g. 'Would you find this in the home?', 'Is this a person?', 'Might I have one of these?', 'Is this something that I can eat?' etc.

5. Work through one example with the whole group e.g. milk — the clue is vegetable, but it also has an animal connection.

6. As the pupils ask their questions spend some time correcting any inappropriate questions e.g. 'What colour is it?' cannot have a yes/no answer; 'Is it the queen?' is a wild guess etc.

7. The first team choose their word and the second team begin the questioning process. The pupils in the first team answer the questions but need to understand that the teacher is the final arbitrator.

8. Points may be awarded for each word successfully or unsuccessfully found.

9. With younger or less able pupils the categorisation can be modified to narrow the field. The initial clue can reflect this e.g. 'Something that you find in the classroom', 'an animal', 'a person' etc.

NOTICES AND SIGNS

The objective of this lesson is to make pupils aware of the importance of 'social sight' signs.

1. Explain to the pupils that notices and signs are there for a purpose and as such are of great importance. They give information and instructions as well as warnings.

2. Give some examples of the different types of signs or notices stressing the health and safety aspects e.g. DANGER — OVERHEAD CABLES, POISON — DO NOT TOUCH, KEEP OUT, but also drawing attention to the information characteristics such as road signs, bus timetables, publicity posters etc.

3. Ask pupils for examples of signs and notices from their own environment and the purpose of each one.

4. Write one of the following lists on the board and ask the pupils to write down where they may expect to find these signs. They may give more than one answer if they wish.

5. List A is suitable for younger or less able pupils, list B requires a greater level of comprehension.

List A

KEEP OUT

THIS WAY

POISON

EXIT

PAY HERE

NO CYCLING

DO NOT TOUCH

PUSH

CLOSED

DANGER

List B

BEWARE OF THE DOG

USE THE FOOTPATH

DO NOT FEED THE ANIMALS

NO STANDING UPSTAIRS

CLOSED UNTIL 2PM

QUEUE THIS SIDE

SLOW DOWN

P (i.e. Parking)

MORNING SERVICE AT 9AM

NO ENTRY

5. The pupils should now make their own list of ten signs or notices, saying where each is to be found, its importance and whether it gives information, instruction or warning.

6. The lesson can be extended or followed up with the pupils making signs with card and felt tip pens, laying out the wording and presenting in a style to capture the attention of those for whom it is intended.

SECRET CODES

The objective of this lesson is to practice basic literacy skills.

1. Write the following coded message on the board
'One day I will be am doctor and your mother is teacher for ever today'

2. Ask if anyone can make sense of this 'sentence' or message.

3. Explain that you are using a code and that the real message is discovered by reading only every third word.

4. Write up the second message
'You we will are make going two to sentences write from secret this messages writing'

5. When the pupils decode this double message they will know that they are going to try the activity for themselves.

6. To begin with ask all pupils to encode this message using every fourth word
'Meet me at midnight outside the back door'

7. Each pupil is then asked to make up their own coded message using this method or some close variation.

8. Pupils are paired up as they complete their work to decode each other's messages.

9. If time permits an extension of this activity is for pupils to invent their own word-based coding systems e.g. syllabic or digraph insertion to each word, word or syllable reversals, splitting word in different places, a continuous string of letters and so on.

3

Working It Out (Maths and Science)

THE ANSWER IS . . .

The objectives of this lesson are to practice basic mathematical computation and also to encourage lateral thinking in setting problems rather than merely solving them.

1. Explain to the class that this will be a maths lesson with a slight difference. Instead of the teacher setting the problems and the pupils finding the answers, they will be given the answer first and they will be able to set their own problems.

2. They will be asked to think up several problems which all have the given answer as their solution.

3. Begin with an example such as 'The answer is five, what is the question?'

4. Explain some of the different types of 'sums' that might be used to reach this answer. This will vary from class to class depending on their age and/or ability level.

5. Some suggestions include simple addition, subtraction, compound addition & subtraction, multiplication, division, compounds of any or all of these, money, fractions, decimals, length, time, volume, area, percentages, as well as problems in a written form rather than in a mathematical formula.

6. It may again be necessary to offer a limited number of examples.

7. The pupils can work at the task individually, in pairs, or in small groups.

8. After a period of time e.g. ten minutes on one answer, the questions can be exchanged with another pupil, pair or group to check that each 'sum' gives the prescribed answer.

9. Another number can be chosen and the exercise repeated.

10. For younger or less able pupils simple whole numbers, usually fairly small, will be appropriate, whilst older or more able pupils will manage larger numbers, fractions or perhaps decimals.

11. The answers must primarily be the correct number. It does not matter whether it is five seconds, five apples, five cm., or five frogs!

FIND THE WORD

The objective of this exercise is to practice basic mathematical computations to solve a word puzzle.

1. Assign each letter of the alphabet with a number A-1, B-2, C-3 etc. (It may be necessary to write this on to the board, but ideally each pupil should work it out on their own paper.)

2. To find the word the pupils need to solve various computational problems and translate the number to its corresponding letter.

3. The problems are increasingly difficult so that pupils can work at their own level. The solutions form words and a phrase.

4. The two parallel lists are for different levels of ability.

List 1	**List 2**	**Solution/Letter**	
$4+3$	$14\div2$	7	G
$7+8$	$30\div2$	15	O
$3+9$	$36\div3$	12	L
$10-6$	$20\div5$	4	D
$12-7$	$30\div6$	5	E
$9-3+8$	$42\div3$	14	N
$5+8+4$	$(3\times7)-4$	17	Q
$10+6+5$	$(6\times4)-3$	21	U
$8+4-3$	$(5\times3)-6$	9	I
$7+9+6+4$	$(8\times4)-6$	26	Z

List 1	List 2	Solution/Letter	
2×3	(10÷5)+4	6	F
3×5	(30÷6)×3	15	O
6×3	(44÷4)+7	18	R
9÷3	1.6+1.4	3	C
16÷2	2/3 of 12	8	H
(4×2)−7	(5×3)−(2×7)	1	A
(3×4)+1	(7×4)−(3×5)	13	M
(5×4)−4	4/5 of 20	16	P
(16÷2)+1	3/2 × 6	9	I
(3×6)−3	7.5×2	15	O
(4×5)−6	(55÷11)+(3×3)	14	N
(6×4)−5	(7×5)−(4×4)	19	S

5. Other problems can be set at different levels or to practice a particular type of 'sum'.

WORKING WITH TRIANGLES

The objective of this lesson is to explore some of the characteristics and properties of the triangle.

Additional materials required include rulers, pencils, paper (preferably squared), scissors.

1. Depending on the age and ability of the pupils it may be necessary to demonstrate either on the board or with a sheet of paper. However, if the pupils are able to understand verbal instructions there are useful teaching points to be made in this approach.

2. The pupils are required to draw a square with sides of 20cm., and are reminded of the properties of a square before beginning, i.e. sides of equal length joined at right angles to each other. If squared paper is not available, a practical suggestion to try and keep the shape regular is to begin at the bottom left hand corner of the sheet of paper and measure 20cm. upwards and across.

3. The remaining two sides can then be drawn from these marks, parallel to the left hand side and bottom of the sheet respectively. This can be gauged by eye fairly accurately, although any problems with poor visual discrimination can be overcome by simply folding the paper from the two marks and marking where the opposite corner touches the paper. This should then form an accurate square. If pupils cannot measure with a ruler then the latter method can be used using the full width of the paper to determine side length (see diagram).

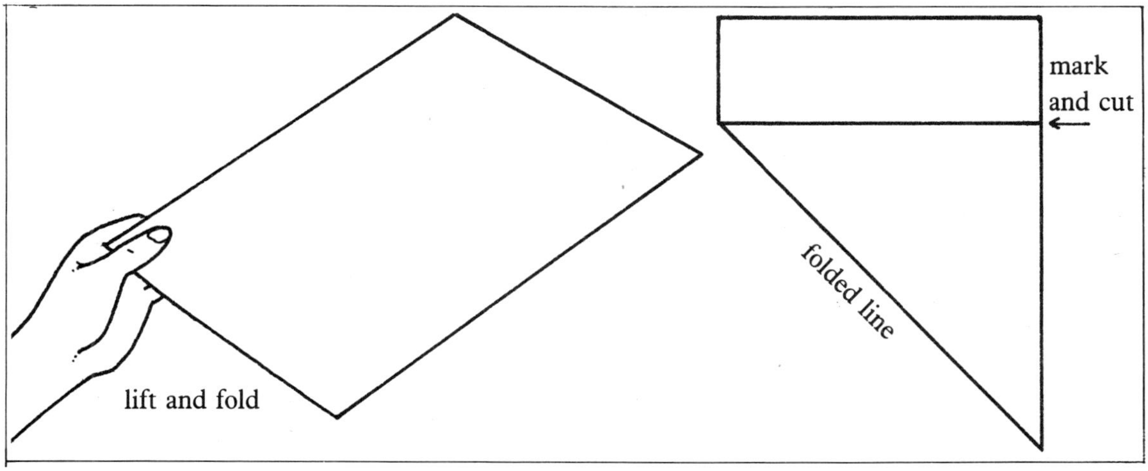

4. The pupils should now cut out their squares.

5. The next stage involves dividing the square diagonally with a ruler, and then repeating the exercise from the opposite corners. The pupils should then be asked to measure half way along each side, make a mark, and then join the marks on opposite sides of the square. The large square should then be cut along these lines, which should provide each pupil with 8 small triangles of the same shape and size.

6. A discussion of these triangles can highlight their main features i.e. 3 sides and 3 angles, one of which is a right angle. The pupils should then be asked to create certain regular shapes with these triangles. Some suggestions are given below ranging from simple to more complex depending on the mathematical knowledge of the pupils.

Small Shapes:

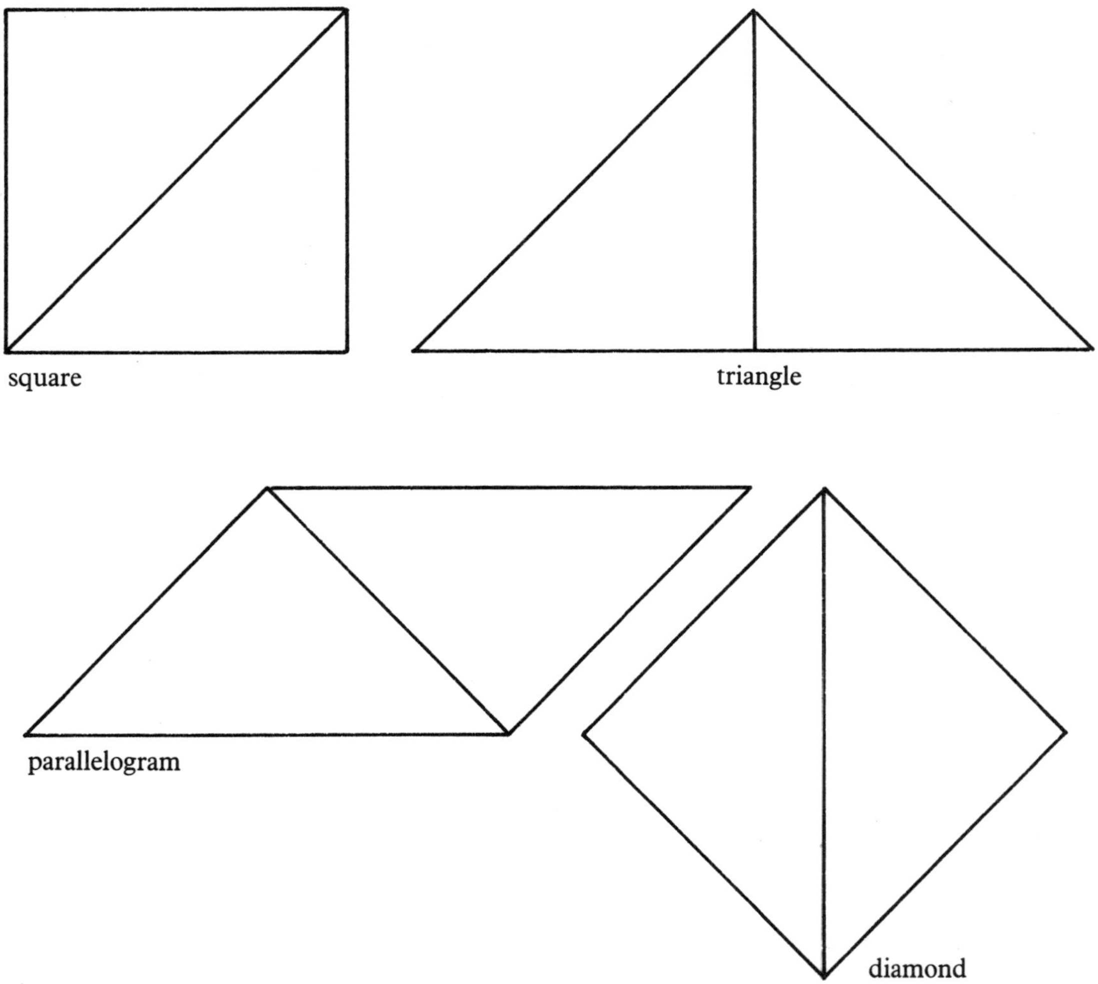

Medium/Large Shapes:

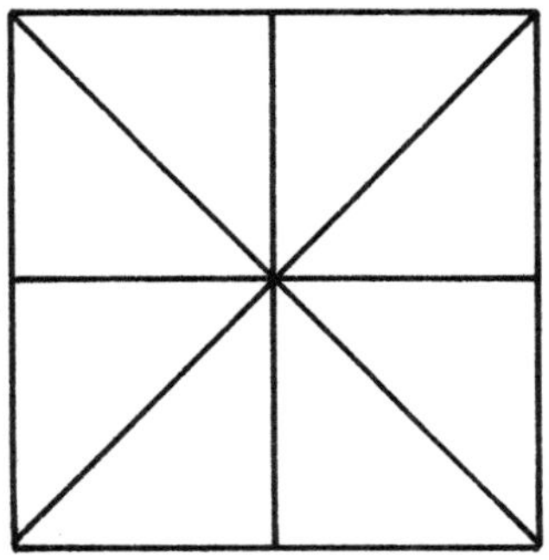

square

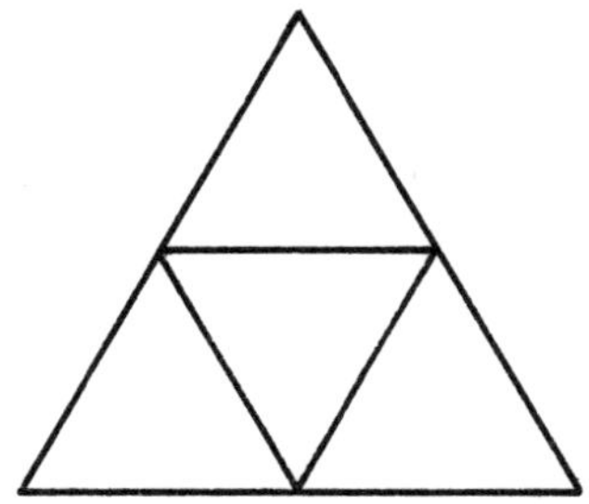

triangle

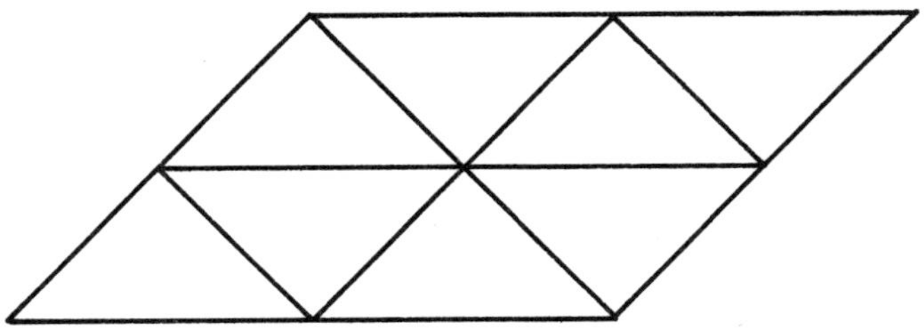

parallelogram

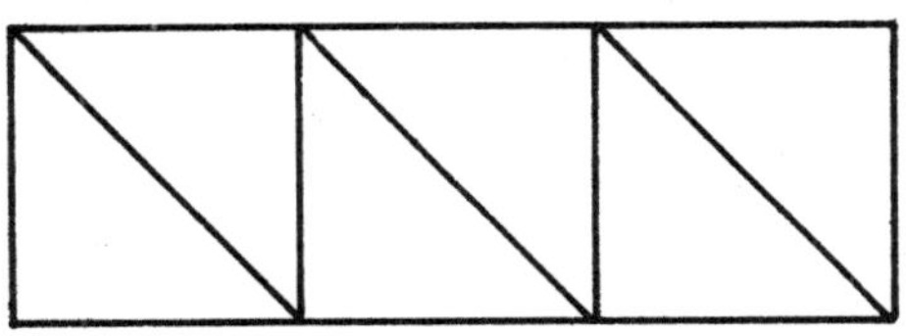

rectangle

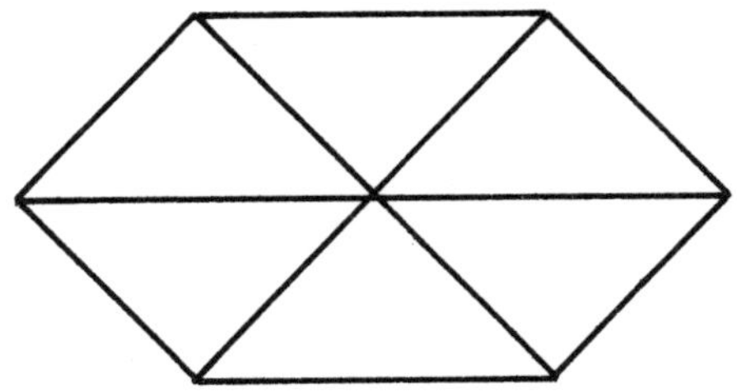

hexagon

7. The pupils are then asked to create their own pictures or patterns using the triangles. These can include house, tree, star, kite and yacht.

8. If it is appropriate, and the group wish to do so, a simple display can be made incorporating both geometric shapes and other creations. These can be glued on to larger pieces of paper (which also means that the quicker workers have to go back to the start again!). Coloured paper, or colouring-in greatly enhances this work.

BAR GRAPHS

The main teaching objective is to demonstrate distribution in a graphical format, which is readily understandable to low achieving pupils.

(It would be helpful if squared graph paper were available.)

1. Explain to the pupils the nature and function of bar graphs i.e. that is the higher a particular column, the greater is the incidence of that commodity or occurrence. Also that like functions can be compared alongside each other.

2. Give an example on the board identifying the number on the vertical axis, and the category on the horizontal axis. A readily available example within the room is the months of the year in which pupils have their birthdays.

3. Draw the axes and begin to fill in one block at a time to demonstrate how the bar graph builds up. The pupils can copy this example on to their own worksheets. They may even come to the board to fill in their own block on the master copy if this is appropriate.

4. Ask the pupils questions about the bar graph when completed on the board — e.g. 'In which month do most pupils have a birthday?' 'In which month do no pupils have a birthday?' 'Are there more birthdays in May or July?' 'When is Mary's birthday?' How many birthdays are there in September?'

5. Divide the class into pairs or small groups. They are then set to undertake a survey of their own of the other pupils in the class to make a bar graph.

6. They may wish to suggest their own themes for this but some suggestions might include favourite food, colour, pop group (these may need to offer a limited choice including a category for none of these'). Other ideas are number of siblings; number or type of pet; colour of eyes/hair clothing item etc.; form of transport used to come to school, as well as many other readily accessible facts, pieces of information or opinions.

7. If time permits the group may wish to share the results of their surveys with others, and this would encourage interpretation of the results.

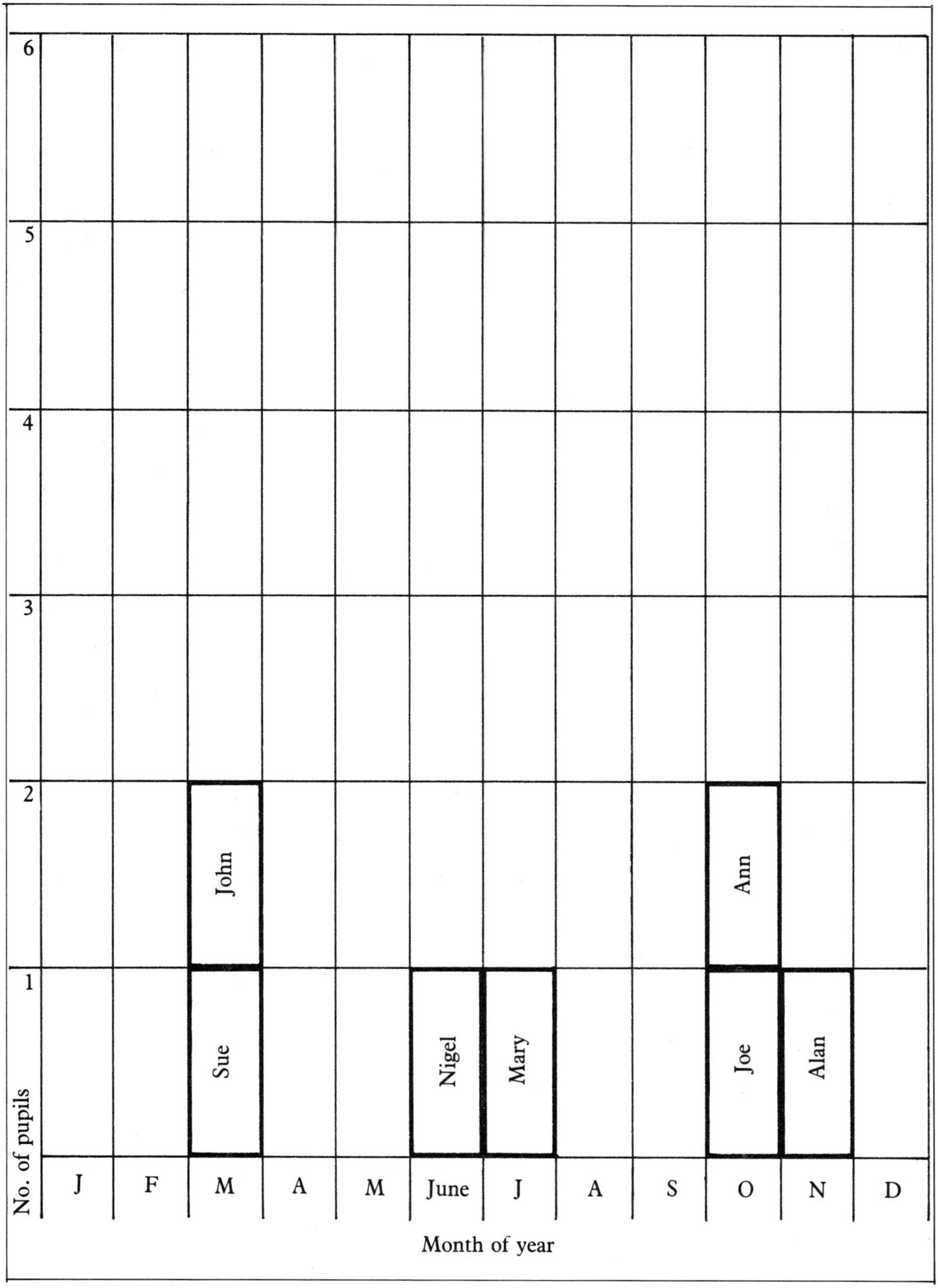

6
5
4
3
2
1
No. of pupils
John
Sue
Nigel
Mary
Ann
Joe
Alan
J
F
M
A
M
June
J
A
S
O
N
D
Month of year

MEASURING

The objective of this lesson is to give a perspective to the use of standard measurements.

1. Introduce the lesson by explaining to the pupils that in the past people have measured distances by using readily available measures for reference.

2. In this way they know that if something is five measures in length it is longer than something which is four measures of the same type. For many purposes this is still the case, for example if you wish to know if a cupboard will fit through a door you do not need a measuring tape, but merely a piece of string or length of wood marked to the width of the cupboard and fitted for size in the doorway.

3. We still have measures which refer back to the days when measuring was a less exact science, for instance horses are measured in 'hands', the 'foot' is a standard (though non-metric) measure which is still widely used.

4. Pupils are asked to measure certain objects using some measures which are readily available.

   a. shorter classroom objects such as books, pencil, paper using the thumb from tip to first joint.

   b. medium sized classroom furniture such as desks, table and chairs using the width of the palm.

   c. larger items around the classroom such as cupboard, door, windows using the hand span (tip of thumb to tip of little finger fully outstretched.)

   d. distances on the floor such as the length and width of the classroom, the width of the corridor using the length of the foot heel to toe successively.

   e. longer distances on the floor such as the length of the corridor, the length and width of the playground using stride length.

5. The pupils can record their results — 'The corridor is 15 strides long, it is 12 times my foot's length (just over two strides) wide'.

6. They may also represent their results diagrammatically if they are capable.

7. If they are able to use measuring implements such as rulers or tape measures their 'ad hoc' measurements can be translated into centimetres and metres.

8. More able or older pupils may try to convert the spans to actual distances using metric measurement, but also using feet, inches and yards to see if there may be any relationship between the original measures used with the introduction of a standard measuring system.

9. The pupils may go on to measure each other and make a height chart. They can also compare hand widths, length of feet and so on.

SPENDING MONEY

The objective of this lesson is to help the pupils understand the requirements of budgetary consideration when dealing with money.

1. Write up on the board a price list, using simple diagrams to represent the products if the pupils' reading abilities are severely limited.

2. The price lists are as follows

sweet shop	**grocery**	**greengrocery**
chocolate bar 20p	baked beans 15p	potatoes 10p lb
lollipop 5p	bread 30p	tomatoes 25p lb
chews 1p ea.	milk 20p pt.	apples 20p lb
crisps 15p	cheese 25p	oranges 10p ea.
can of pop 15p	margarine 20p lb	carrots 15p lb
box of sweets 50p	pizza 35p ea.	onions 5p lb

3. The pupils are 'going shopping' with certain amounts of money to spend e.g. 30p in the sweetshop, £1.20 in the grocers, 75p in the greengrocers.

4. They are to write down how they spend the money allocated, and any change that they might have left.

5. A variation might involve buying items in each shop with a limited overall budget.

6. A further variation would be to ask the pupils direct questions such as 'If I have 20p and buy a packet of crisps how much change would I have?'; 'If I buy two pizzas and a bottle of milk how much will it cost, or how much change would I have from £1?'; 'If I have 50p and buy a pound of tomatoes and a pound of carrots what fruit can I afford?'.

7. More able or older pupils could also be set specific tasks e.g. buy a snack meal including a drink for £1 or less; buy ingredients for a cooked meal for two for £1.80 or less; buy sweets to share between three children for 40p; plus other variations appropriate to the particular pupils.

8. Younger pupils might also enjoy acting out a shopping expedition.

LIVING THINGS

The objective of this lesson is to give the pupils an appreciation of the basic requirements for life to continue.

1. Living things can take many forms. It may be plant life or trees, insects or fish. There are many very primitive animal forms as well as higher orders of animals including humans.

2. The four basic characteristics of living things are that they need to have food and oxygen. They also need to have young and to grow.

3. Ideally this information should be given by the pupils through judicious questioning and discussion.

4. There are many forms of different classifications for living things, dependent on criteria. For practical purposes it will be suitable to make three lists. Plant life (including trees, shrubs, flowers, fungi); invertebrates (without a backbone) including insects, crustaceans, spiders; and vertebrates (animals with backbones).

5. The vertebrates can be divided into fish, amphibian, reptile, bird and mammal. These each have their own characteristics. Fish live in water and have scales and gills to take in oxygen from water. Amphibians have soft damp skin, have young born in the water, and can also move on land. Reptiles live on land and have scaly skin. Birds have feathers and scaly feet and lay eggs — they can usually, but not always, fly. Mammals have live babies, feed their young with milk, and have skin with hair.

6. This information can be given or elicited through discussion. It should then be noted on the board along with examples of the three lists.

7. A useful exercise is to ask the pupils questions to ensure that they have understood the content of the lesson. The information on the board acts as an aide-memoire and also helps with spelling.

8. Questions can be given at any level dependent on the age and ability of the pupils. Typical questions might be 'Name two animals with backbones'; 'Is a fish a mammal?'; 'Is a mushroom a living thing?'; 'What is the difference between a reptile and an amphibian?'; 'What are the four needs of living things?'.

9. Pupils can draw pictures to depict these four needs.

10. Pupils may wish to investigate further how plants reproduce (apart from seeds), or how different living things take in their food and oxygen.

4

Do-It-Yourself (Creative Activities)

CHARADES

The objectives of this lesson are to encourage dramatic expression and lateral thinking in the interpretation of words.

1. 'Charades' is the traditional parlour game in which clues are given in mime to help identify a word or phrase. It has been popularised in the television programme 'Give Us a Clue'.

2. The clues are usually based on the categories of book, film, song title or television programme. There is a recognised standard mime for each of the categories.

3. The number of words in the phrase is indicated with the fingers of the right hand, and the word being mimed is indicated with the corresponding finger.

4. For more sophisticated mime, the number of syllables in a particular word are indicated by the fingers of the right hand on the left forearm, with the particular syllable being mimed indicated by the corresponding finger.

5. Small link words such as *the*, *an*, *a*, *and*, and *is* are indicated by holding the thumb and first finger of the right hand about 1 cm. apart.

6. A mime of the whole phrase is indicated by describing a circle with both hands.

7. The group is divided into teams of four or five. If necessary they can have two games with the more successful teams playing each other second time around.

8. One player is chosen from the first team and is given a phrase in one of the categories to mime to his/her own team.

9. Each mime must be done either word by word or as a whole until the whole phrase has been guessed by the rest of the team. A time limit of two or three minutes is probably required.

10. Correct solutions to the mime are awarded one point. Verbal clues are forbidden and the teacher referees to ensure fair play!

11. The game continues until each player has had their turn at a mime.

12. It is probably better if the teacher sets the clues as this assures some standardisation. However, it may be decided to allow the groups to set clues to challenge each other. A few suggestions for clues include 'The Good, the Bad and the Ugly'; 'Eastenders'; 'Oliver Twist'; 'Goldfinger'.

IMPROVISATIONS

The objectives of this lesson are to improve verbal expression and encourage dramatic expression.

1. First of all ask the pupils if they are familiar with the word 'improvisation'. If they are then proceed with the lesson, if not take a minute or two to explain the meaning of the term in dramatic activities.

2. Explain to those who do not know the term that improvisation is in its simplest meaning making up a play or scene as you go along. It is the spontaneous response to a situation emerging unexpectedly.

3. 'Improvisation' also acts as a vehicle for exploring situations and feelings in an unthreatening, imaginary situation.

4. Divide the class into small groups of three or four pupils. Give them a scenario or theme and allow them to discuss this for about 15 or 20 minutes. During this time the pupils are asked to begin improvising the scene.

5. Whilst this is taking place move among the groups offering help and suggestions in setting up and running the improvisations. Many pupils are wary of speaking out if this is not a familiar exercise, but they need to be encouraged to do so. It helps if roles are decided within the groups so that characters and/or opinions can begin to form.

6. Any imaginary (or even real) scene may form the basis for an improvisation. Some suggestions are

   a. stealing from home and being found out
   b. being sent to the headteacher for something that you didn't do.
   c. a bank robbery
   d. booking a holiday in a travel agency
   e. coming home late to angry parents
   f. going to the doctor's
   g. helping an injured person
   h. being offered drugs at a party
   i. seeing someone shoplifting
   j. going out for a meal to a restaurant

7. After the time allotted to prepare the improvisation the groups may wish to perform for the rest of the group. These performances are unlikely to take more than a few minutes each.

8. There may be a general group discussion on the theme looking at the feelings and actions of the characters, questioning their motives/opinions to ask how reasonable they are.

9. Alternatively if the groups do not wish to perform to each other another scene or topic may be introduced.

FLAGS AND COATS-OF-ARMS

The objective of this lesson is to promote original thought in creative artwork.
Additional equipment to the standard pencil and paper would ideally include art paper and crayons or other colouring materials.

1. Introduce the lesson by explaining that flags and coats-of-arms are commonly used to identify nations, towns, associations and clubs, even individual families.

2. Depending on the age and ability level of the pupils and how structured you would like the lesson to be, determine which type of flag, crest, emblem or coat-of-arms the pupils are going to make.

3. Generally speaking national flags, either real or imagined, are easier since they are rectangular, usually with simple mathematical patterns. They can form an impressive display.

4. Crests, emblems, coats-of-arms for a town, club, association or heraldic purposes are usually much more complicated since their shape is rarely regular (often based on a shield symbol — see example layout below), and often includes a motto or phrase of some description. This gives a great deal more scope for imaginative thinking and interpretation.

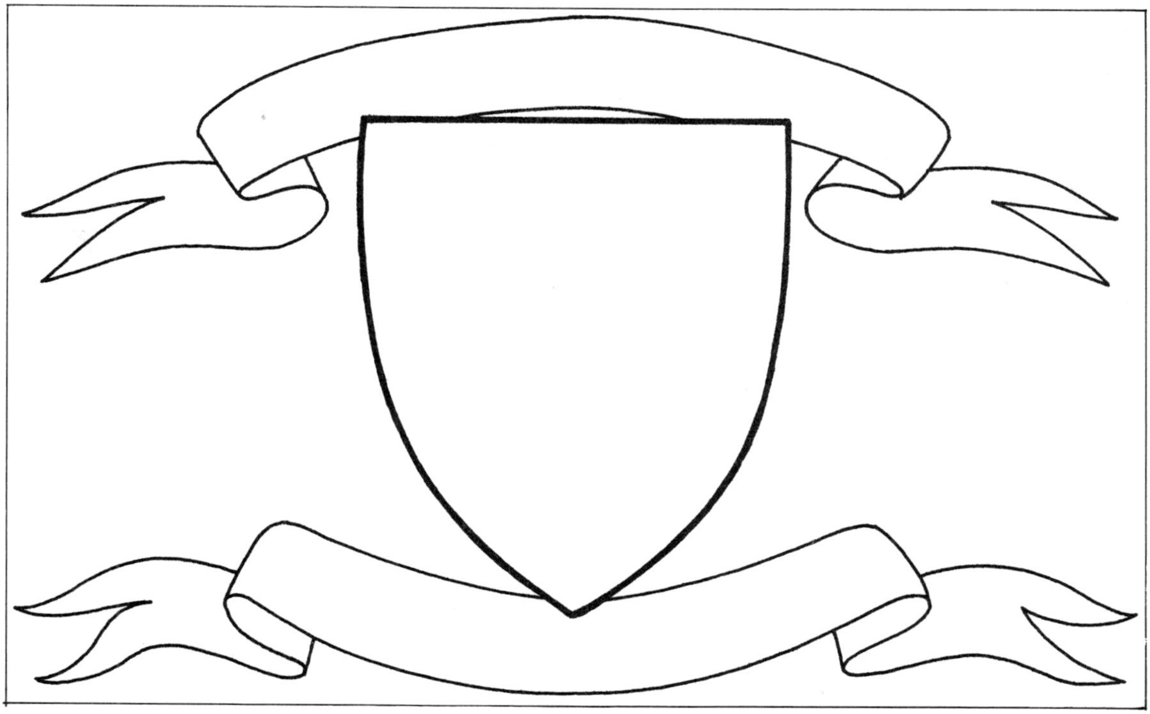

5. Having decided on the type of activity to be undertaken it is a good idea if the pupils now begin work on a rough draft. If this is suitable the pupils may now move on to complete their piece of work.

6. Suggestions may be based on something with which the pupil is already familiar, but copying directly e.g. from a blazer badge should be discouraged, or even disallowed.

7. General group discussion may elicit ideas as to the appropriate type of emblem for a particular badge or coat-of-arms. For instance an optician may incorporate glasses into his family crest, the Union of Mineworkers may depict a helmet and winding gear into their banner, or a town crest may incorporate a particular feature such as the local castle.

8. Older pupils may wish to design a family coat-of-arms to include something relevant to their personal family circumstances or history. They may possibly highlight their own aspirations and hopes for adulthood and future employment either in the crest or the motto.

9. The possibilities are only boundaried by the imagination of the pupils and their artistic ability. In any case work completed should be displayed if the pupils so wish.

MAKING MASKS

The objective of the lesson is somewhat dependent on the content. In the first suggested activity it is to encourage creativity and imagination, in the second activity it is also to explore emotions through facial expressions.

Additional equipment required for this lesson includes thin card or strong white cartridge paper, scissors, string, and colouring materials such as crayons or felt-tip pens.

1. The first activity is for **younger or less able pupils** and involves the making of a 'theme' mask. Various themes can be used — futuristic, monster, pirate, witch or wizard.

2. The pupils begin by drawing the outline shape of the mask, and this may vary considerably depending on the theme chosen. When this is deemed satisfactory they cut out the shape and proceed to fill in the background and the features (if there are any).

3. This is a fairly lengthy process and should not be rushed to completion. However, when it is satisfactorily completed holes can be made at either side and string inserted. This when adjusted to length should enable the maker to wear the mask.

4. Masks essentially provide the opportunity for an alter ego and dramatic activities may well ensue, especially with younger pupils.

5. **Older or more able pupils** can make masks in the style of the Ancient Greeks. These portray emotions and were worn throughout plays in the Greek theatre.

6. In this case the masks are cut to a standard shape which can be drawn in advance on the board.

7. It may also be necessary to explain to the pupils the function of the features in determining a stylised expression of emotion e.g. downturned mouth indicates sadness whilst an upturned mouth denotes happiness; arched eyebrows and an open mouth denote surprise whilst furrowed eyebrows with a downturned mouth indicate anger; a furrowed brow indicates thoughtfulness, worry or concern.

8. This analysis of facial expressions is a useful exercise in itself, but having talked of the possibilities, and perhaps having seen a few examples on the board, the pupils are now asked to make a mask of their own.

9. The procedure is similar to that previously given, but a more suitable medium may be soft lead pencil on to the white card or paper.

10. Here again the masks may stimulate some dramatic activity, possibly in small groups. There is also the possibility of analysing the expressions to see if they have achieved what was intended, and if not how the features might have been altered to do so.

QUICK ON THE DRAW

The object of this lesson is to encourage pupils to draw representationally in order that their colleagues might identify the meaning in the drawing.

1. Explain to the pupils that they are going to play a game which involves representing a word or a phrase by means of a drawing.

2. This can be very simple for less able pupils using only nouns of common objects such as horse, aeroplane, tulip, or simple verbs e.g. kicking, flying, ski-ing.

3. To begin with the teacher can demonstrate by drawing something suitable on the board with the pupils guessing.

4. The pupils can then be divided into two teams of equal size, and if possible roughly equal ability.

5. One member of each team in turn is asked to come to the board and is given a word or short phrase which must be represented pictorially.

6. One point is awarded to the artist's team for each correct guess.

7. The teacher sets the clue on each occasion, and this can be tailored to the capability of each individual pupil.

8. It is usually a good idea for the clues to begin as fairly easy, then to get progressively more difficult as the game proceeds, and as the pupils become more confident in their willingness to draw.

9. Any words or phrases can be used at the teacher's discretion, but it may be valuable to think in terms of a theme game using something like popular film titles (Around the World in 80 days, Star Wars etc.). Other themes might be foreign countries, TV programmes, titles of pop songs or pop groups.

10. Extra points may be awarded for 'artistic interpretation' and originality of thought or expression.

5

Looking at Life (Social Studies)

A BALANCED DIET

The objectives of this lesson are an awareness of balance in diet and the need for nutrition.

1. Begin with a general discussion on the need for food, the effects of going without it whether by choice or otherwise (anorexia, poverty, punishment).

2. Having established that food is a vital requirement to the maintenance of life and growth, discuss the dietary content in the west, the third world and widely differing cultures.

3. Try to elicit responses as to whether all food is good for you, or if you can indeed have too much of a good thing.

4. At this point the group should now be discussing basic dietary considerations such as eating too much 'junk' food, stodgy food or simply eating too much (or too little).

5. Explain to the class that they are going to design a menu for one day, comprising of breakfast, snack lunch and cooked evening meal. It is not an exercise watching calories too carefully, but rather offering a balanced diet for healthy (and pleasurable!) eating.

6. The class can divide into small groups of three or four to promote discussion on the topic. The pupils may decide to write their own menus, or they may compile a joint menu, perhaps with some element of choice to indicate that not everyone likes the same thing.

7. The criteria for the main meal is that there should be a starter, a main course with vegetables and a sweet.

8. It may be a useful exercise for some pupils to discuss the type of food that may be considered as a starter.

9. Once the pupils have completed the set activity they can discuss the menus chosen within the larger group.

10. Drinks are also an important part of the balanced diet and should be included throughout the exercise.

11. An interesting challenge may also be for pupils to plan a vegetarian menu for a day.

12. An extension of the activity might involve a dramatic interpretation of a meal out at a restaurant or a conflict at mealtime at home (see lesson on page 55 'Improvisations').

13. A further exercise includes classification of food by various criteria. If the pupils are given a list of various foods they can subdivide them as meat, vegetable, fruit, cereal, sweet foods, home-grown, 'foods I like/dislike', 'foods that are good/bad for me' and many other categorisations. This should help the pupils to look more critically into the food they eat.

FAVOURITE TV PROGRAMMES

The objective of this lesson is to encourage pupils to critically analyse television programmes and their own viewing habits.

1. Begin with a discussion of some general categories of TV programmes. Suggestions to work towards are game shows, documentaries, news and current affairs, plays, sport, soaps, music, films, educational and entertainment.

2. Identify a few programmes in each category as examples, and list on the board.

3. Ask if pupils have a preference for particular types of programme. Undertake a mini-survey and note the results alongside the categories listed.

4. Do likewise with programme categories which the pupils dislike.

5. Determine general reasons for the likes and dislikes and note this in summary form alongside the other information. Typical examples of reasons might be that the programme is action-packed, fast-moving, interesting, well acted, too much talking — too little action, good/bad background music.

6. Dependent on the results either

a. Compare the types of programme within one category. List the good and bad points of different programmes e.g. soaps — an American may be deemed low in terms of realism, but high in terms of story and acting; a locally produced programme may be more realistic, but lack the glamour of American soaps or alternatively

b. Ask pupils to make a list of one programme in each category that they like and dislike.

Category	**Favourite Programme**	**Least favourite programme**
game show		
documentary		
news/current affairs		
soap		
play		
sport		
music		
films		
educational		
entertainment		

7. If time permits pupils can write down the name of their favourite programme. The category into which it falls and the reasons why it is their chosen favourite. In addition they may also be asked to suggest ways in which this programme might be improved.

8. As an extension to this activity pupils may form into small groups as 'panel members' and be called on to offer opinions of various television programmes.

HEADLINES

The objective of this lesson is to encourage critical thinking and analysis of newspaper articles.

One or more newspapers (preferably tabloid) are required for this lesson.

1. Choose a fairly uninformative banner headline and read it out. Ask the pupils for their opinions as to the content of the article.

2. After a brief discussion on this theme read out the first few paragraphs of the article which usually encapsulate the core of the story and see how close were the guesses.

3. Now read out the first few paragraphs of another article and ask the pupils to suggest possible headlines for the story. Encourage a variety of guesses reminding pupils of the humourous or whimsical type of headline, and the frequent use of puns and other figures of speech.

4. Read out the actual headline to see if anyone guessed correctly and discuss whether any of the suggestions were better than the original caption, and if so why they were.

5. Continue the lesson by providing further headlines either real or created, and ask the pupils to make up a story to fit the headline. They can write this down, or if this is beyond their literacy abilities tell the story to the class.

6. Alternatively give a brief outline of a news story (human interest themes are usually popular), and ask the pupils for a headline.

7. Suggestions for this further work include a child locked in a shed overnight by accident; a horse loose on the motorway; a high street bank robbery; sporting hooligans loose in a seaside town; students doing a rag week stunt; a vicar riding a motorbike and wearing a leather jacket.

8. Explain to the pupils the importance of presentation of news in this way. The headline has to be eye-catching and take the readers' attention. The first few paragraphs give a brief outline of the story, often in a fairly sensational journalistic style (especially in the tabloids).

9. The remainder of the article fills out the story in a style that is partly determined by the readership of that newspaper and possibly its political persuasion, and partly by that particulár journalist or newspaper's distinctive style.

10. The lesson can develop into a more critical appraisal of these factors only if the pupils have the basic understanding of the concepts involved. If this is the case, despite their learning problems, it may even be possible to discuss how certain issues might be treated in different newspapers dependent on their political persuasion, editor or readership.

ADVERTISING

The objectives of this lesson are to encourage critical analysis of advertisements, and a greater comprehension of the wording of adverts and its expected impact on the consumer.

A selection of adverts from newspapers or magazines would be an advantage with this lesson, though if this is impossible the sample advert can either be photocopied or transcribed on to the board.

1. Discuss with the class the purpose of advertising — primarily to bring a product to the attention of the consumer, usually with the purpose of selling it! Choose examples of adverts to display this as clearly as possible.

2. Identify the various advertising media — TV, commercial radio, hoardings, newspapers, magazines.

3. Look at the way that the message is packaged — usually catchy or gimmicky with jingles or easily identifiable characters on TV and radio; rather more eye-catching in the press and on posters.

4. Focus on product advertising rather than personal or other small ads, or event or political promotional information.

5. If there are newspapers or magazines available get the pupils to find and cut out such adverts. If not focus on the sample advert.

6. Discuss the layout of an advertisement. Look for some analysis of the style of the advert. In the sample advert ask the pupils what is its most striking feature. Is it the name of the product, its price/value for money, its special features, any 'free' gifts or accessories, the terms of sale, the price?

7. What is it that the manufacturers are trying to say when selling their product?

FREE

1 year's supply of
soap powder of
your own choice
(12 economy packs at
est. cost of £30.25)

save
£60
(on machine and
powders - total mrp
£310.25)

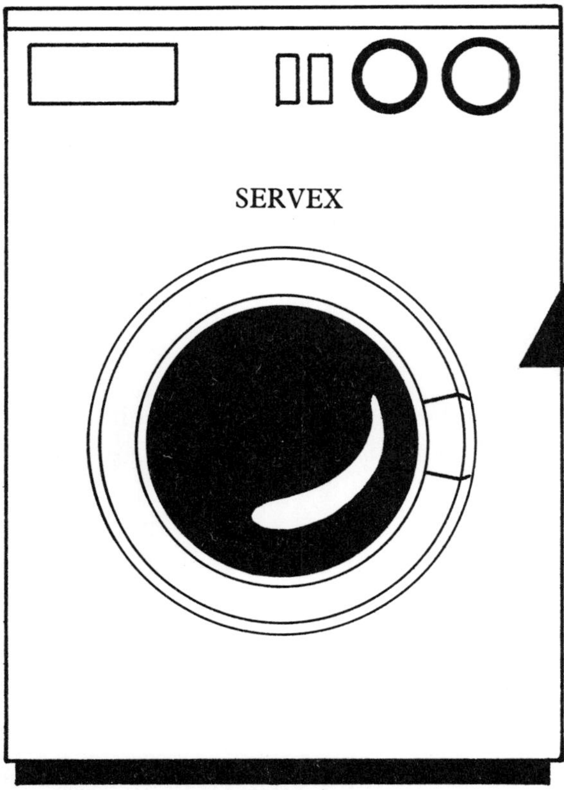

Our price only
£249.95
(credit available
on request)

SERVEX FRONT-LOADING AUTOMATIC

includes
varying spin speed
12 electronically
controlled programmes
'rinse & spin' option

BUY NOW

Limited
offer - closes
on 31st August

8. Ask the pupils the following questions about their advert.
   a. How much does it cost?
   b. Is it always this price?
   c. If not how much is saved?
   d. What do you get extra (if anything)?
   e. Are there any conditions to the sale?
   f. Do you think that this is value for money?
   g. If so, why; if not why not?
   h. Is the advert eye-catching, and why?
   i. Would you buy this product, and why or why not?
   j. Is this advert successful, why and how?

9. Extension activities can include designing an advert, informed choice between products, consumer protection, buying on credit and immoral advertising.

PERSONAL FACTS

The objective of this lesson is to reinforce the importance of knowing personal information for a variety of reasons, but particularly form-filling.

1. Begin by discussing the personal facts that are most frequently asked such as name, address and date of birth.

2. With children or young people these facts, plus other relevant information is usually collected on behalf of the individual and any necessary paperwork completed by an adult.

3. However, as people get older the burden to not only know the information, but also to be able to write it down increases. Adults cannot fulfil a full role in our society unless they are able to fill in forms etc.

4. Ask the pupils what sort of information they might be required to produce about themselves, and in what circumstances, including personal characteristics for a passport or certain jobs. Also personal measurements when shopping for clothes.

5. Write up on the board the following:

Personal Information Form

Names: Surname ______________________________

Forenames ______________________________

Address: ______________________________

Town ______________________________

County ______________________________

Postcode ______________________________

Telephone No.: ______________________________

Date of birth: ______________________ Age: ________

Place of birth: ______________________

Family Doctor (GP) ______________________

Relations: Father's Name ______________________ Age ________

Mother's Name ______________________ Age ________

Name of Brothers & Sisters ______________________ Age ________

______________________ Age ________

______________________ Age ________

______________________ Age ________

Father's Occupation: ______________________

Mother's Occupation: ______________________

(Your) Occupation: ______________________

Height: ______________ Weight: ______________

Colour of eyes: ______________ Colour of hair: ______________

Other distinguishing features: ______________________

Clothing sizes: Waist ______________________

Chest/bust ______________________

Ladies' Dress size ______________________

Shoe size ______________________

Hat size ______________________

Inside leg (men) ______________________

6. This list can be extended endlessly into other areas such as likes and dislikes in food, entertainment, friends, TV, music, sport etc. However, it should be drawn to the pupils' attention that the former information is factual whilst the latter is subjective opinion.

7. Older and more able pupils who are approaching school leaving age can write a letter of application for a job, drawing attention to their personal strengths, and also providing a small amount of relevant personal information.

GOING TO THE DOCTOR

This lesson is a preliminary activity in social and independence skill training.

1. Begin the lesson with a discussion of a visit to the doctor's surgery. Reasons for visiting the doctor vary enormously and some people would visit their GP when others would seek a remedy for an illness from the chemist, or just wait for it to go away naturally.

2. Presuming that you have decided that the illness, injury or medical problem is sufficiently serious to merit a visit to the surgery, the discussion can now focus on the usual sequence on such an occasion.

3. Note the salient points on the board for reference.

4. If the family doctor (or GP) has an appointment system it will be necessary first to make an appointment, though if it is very urgent it is often possible to go along and wait. A visit to the receptionist or a phone call is required to make the appointment with a particular doctor if this is requested.

5. On arrival at the surgery it is usual to check in at reception, then wait in the waiting room until called to the particular doctor's office.

6. On entering the room the patient describes their symptoms or problem to the doctor who sometimes makes an examination and asks further questions in order to determine the appropriate treatment or try to identify and solve the problem.

7. If a prescription is given this needs to be taken to a chemist who usually makes it up with a few minutes wait. Instructions on the container or any advice that the doctor or chemist offer should be followed precisely to ensure rapid recovery.

8. Occasionally patients are referred to consultants for further treatment, or asked to return to the surgery in a specified time. The patient is also expected to help himself or herself in many instances.

9. This resume of a visit to the doctor encompasses many points of social training, and helps to prepare pupils for the real situation when it next arises with a greater awareness of the process. It should also engender lively discussion.

10. This discussion can be followed up by role play in small groups of three or four, involving the characters of patient (with imaginary ailment), receptionist, doctor and chemist (optional).

11. The improvisations arising out of this activity can be performed for the rest of the class.

12. Alternatively the pupils may write a short piece on the theme of 'My visit to the doctor', either real or imagined.

13. The lesson may help to demystify doctors by encouraging the pupils to think of them as caring not awe-inspiring, and to relate to them in a sensible young adult way, describing their own problems accurately and seeking help and advice accordingly.

6

The World Around Us (Humanities)

LIFE WITHOUT ELECTRICITY

The objectives of this lesson are to compare a modern day facility with its absence in the historical past, and to investigate how our ancestors managed without electricity.

1. Explain to the class that nowadays we depend on many things which were not readily available in the past. Look for them to provide examples, and hopefully electricity will be one of these.

2. Electricity is a relatively recent invention.

3. Make a list of everyday items which are electrically operated, including batteries. Note these suggestions on the board perhaps under the broad headings of essential and non-essential items (and this in itself should prove interesting).

4. Ask each pupil to make their own list of electrical items that they used yesterday.

5. Choose two fairly obvious items such as a washing-machine and electric lights and discuss how they might have coped with them before the advent of electricity.

6. Divide the class into groups of three or four to discuss 'A day in the life of. . . .' — the key factor being the absence of electricity.

7. Dependent on the age and/or ability of the pupils and their previous knowledge and teaching of history, suggestions for the above can include 'A day in the life of a caveman, a Viking, one of Jesus' followers, a Crusader, a Roman, a Greek' plus any other as deemed appropriate.

8. The imagined day is to include various aspects of work and leisure such as getting up and preparing for the day, going out to work (or hunt or battle), domestic chores, home entertainment, and transport.

9. The groups should note their observations and report back to the other groups at the end of the lesson.

10. They may also write a descriptive passage on the theme or make a drawing of their imagined scene with modern day electrical gadgets alongside the historical scene.

HISTORICAL FIGURES – GOOD AND BAD

The objective of this lesson is to encourage the pupils to think critically about how history judges its characters.

1. Begin with a general introduction to the topic identifying historical signposts from pre-history to the present day. Briefly mention cave men and the development of civilisation, the ancient Greeks, the Roman Empire (including the life of Jesus), 1066 and the Norman Invasion, the Middle Ages, Victorian Britain and the World Wars.

2. It is also worth highlighting the fact that history is currently being made and citing a few examples of world affairs such as the troubles in Northern Ireland, the famine in Ethiopia, apartheid in South Africa.

3. Explain that history consists of events, but also how certain characters have helped to shape these events.

4. Ask the group to name any historical figures that they know and make a list on the board.

5. Ask the pupils what they know of each character who is mentioned, perhaps with which events they are associated, and the era or dates during which they were alive.

6. Explain that history is a subjective study. There are no definitive viewpoints, only the opinions of historians which often differ widely. History is littered with events which are open to widely differing interpretations. Some may broadly be classified as good or worthwhile (social changes, freedom from slavery), whilst others may be generally deemed bad or futile (natural disasters, genocide, wars?).

7. Similarly historical characters have widely differing reputations. However, some are almost universally regarded as either good or bad.

8. Split the class into small groups with someone nominated to make note of the group's findings.

9. Working from the master list on the board divide the historical characters into good, bad or indifferent. It may be appropriate to use a sliding scale, say five, seven, or nine points to cover the spectrum. Pupils would then have a range of 'badness' or 'goodness'.

10. After about 15 or 20 minutes for discussion the groups report back to the whole class. They must be prepared to defend their 'rating' of any particular character if questioned.

TOWN MAP

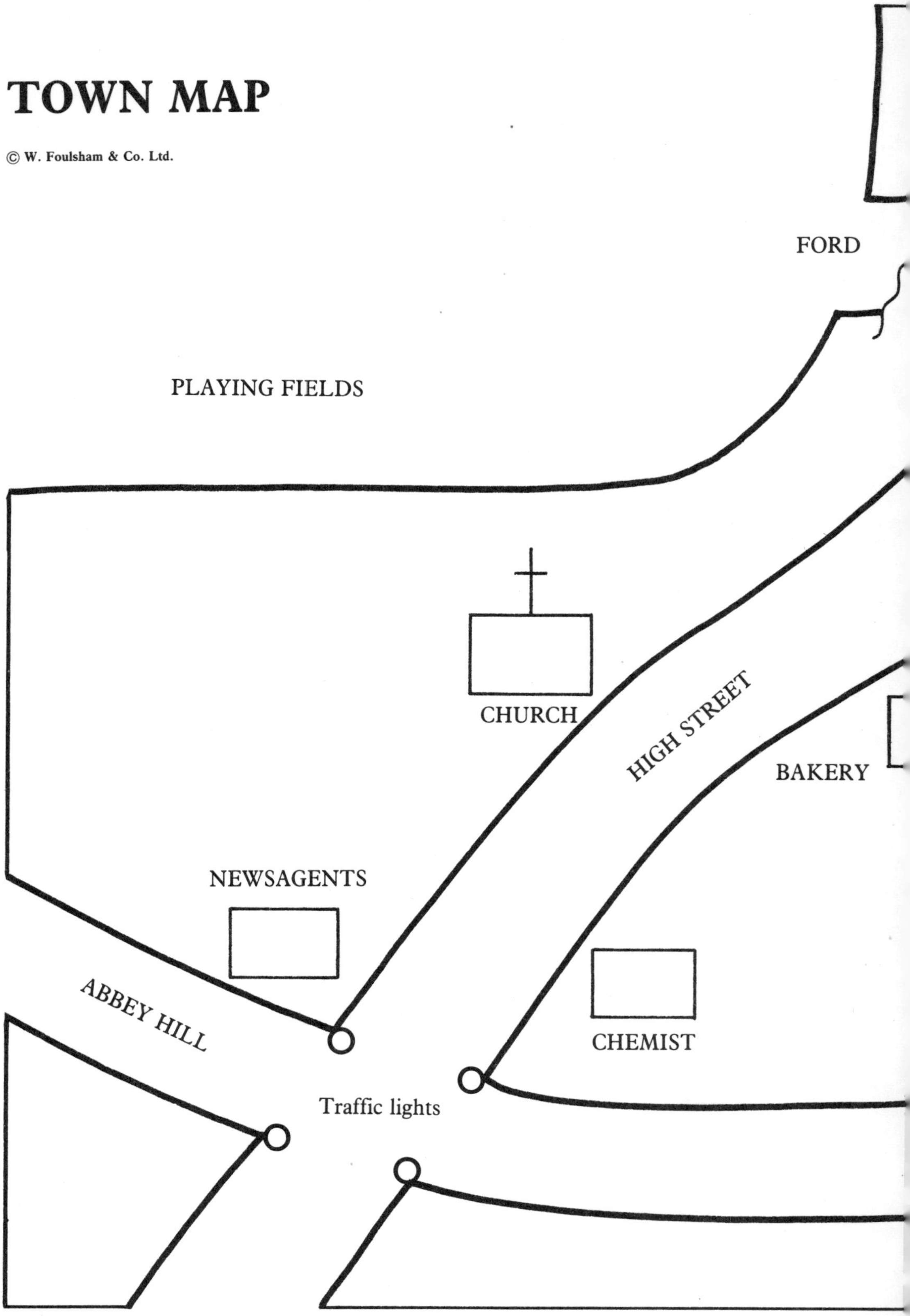
FORD
PLAYING FIELDS
CHURCH
HIGH STREET
BAKERY
NEWSAGENTS
ABBEY HILL
CHEMIST
Traffic lights

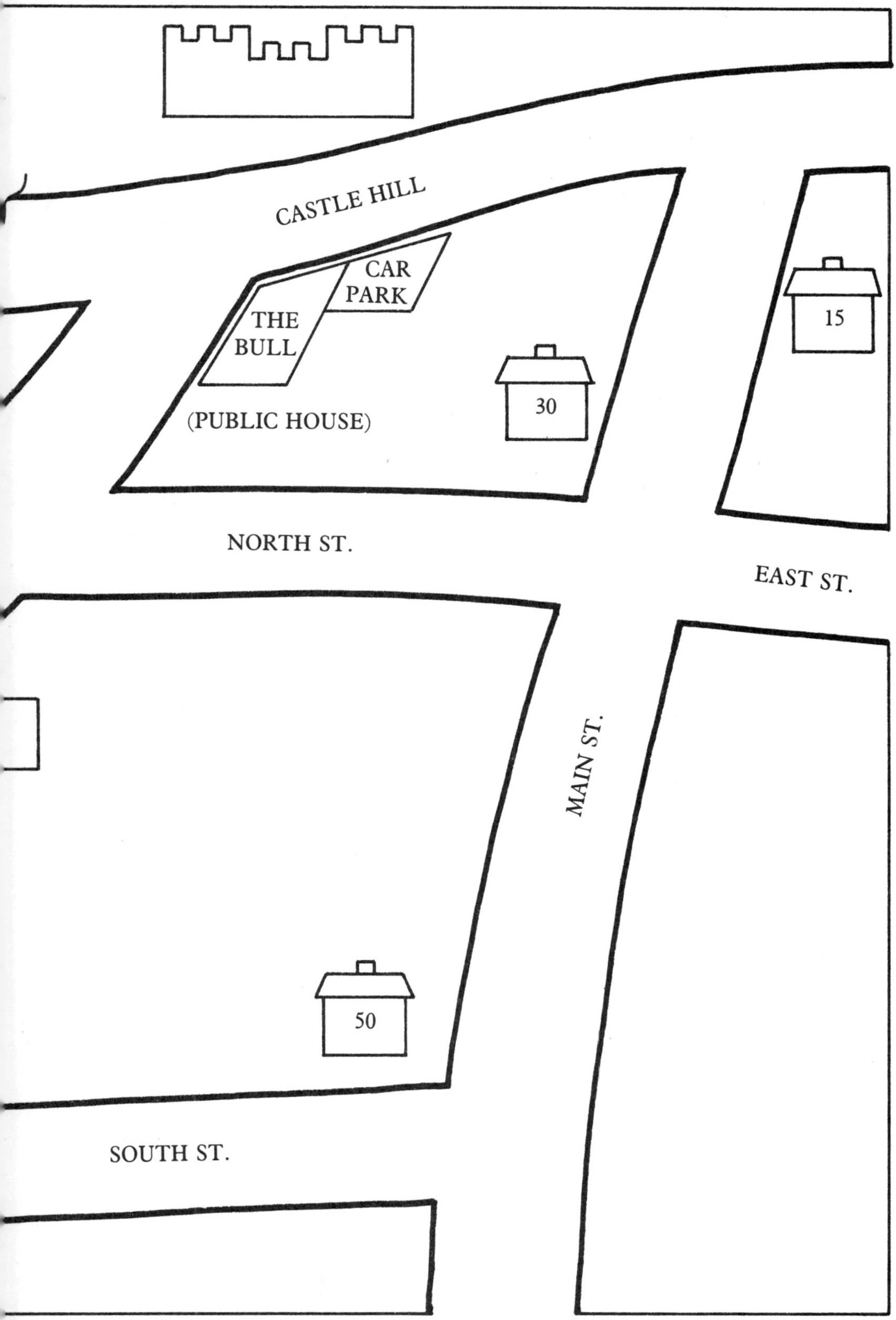
CASTLE HILL
CAR PARK
THE BULL
(PUBLIC HOUSE)
30
15
NORTH ST.
EAST ST.
MAIN ST.
50
SOUTH ST.

MAPS

The objectives of this lesson are to introduce symbolic representation, and teach the pupils to follow directions using a diagrammatic 'map'.

1. Either photocopy the map on the previous page or draw up on to the board and ask the pupils to copy. (The publisher gives permission for this map to be photocopied.
2. Identify with the pupils the various places of interest on the map. Look at the names of the streets, with certain houses identified, buildings which often provide landmarks for direction finding, and the traffic lights and road junctions.

3. Ask the pupils to trace the route as follows with their finger — 'John left his house at number 30 Main St. and turned right out of the house. He then turned right into North St., then left into High St. He turned right at the traffic lights into Abbey Hill where he went into the Newsagent's shop. On the way home he went straight on at the traffic lights into South St. and then left into Main St. where he returned to his house at number 30 with his dad's evening paper.'

4. If some pupils find this difficult it may be necessary to give more examples of a similar nature.

5. Pupils are now asked to describe certain routes e.g. from the playing fields to number 50 South St.; from number 15 Main St. to the church; from the castle to the newsagents.

6. Pupils may describe these routes verbally, or even point them out with their fingers, whilst older or more able pupils may write down the directions for specified routes.

7. Activities to extend this lesson include making similar diagrammatic 'maps' of the classroom, part of the school, the local area around home or school, the journey from home to school, or even the centre of town.

A LAND OF LEISURE

The objective of this lesson is to encourage pupils to think more positively of the natural environment and what it has to offer in terms of leisure activities and pursuits.

1. Begin with a class discussion on places to pursue leisure activities outside the home. Some are created by man such as fairgrounds, cinemas, theatres. Others occur naturally such as the seashore, mountains, caves, rivers and lakes.

2. Ask the pupils to give examples of holidays or trips taken to places created naturally rather than man-made.

3. Make a list of the types of environment mentioned on the board.

4. Ask the pupils, either individually or in groups, to make a list of leisure pursuits and activities relevant to one or more of the naturally occurring environments. For hills this may include fell-walking, hiking, hang-gliding, camping, potholing, bird watching and so on.

5. The groups can come together to compare notes on the variety of activities that are available in the natural environment.

6. Look for the value of this type of holiday or trip, as opposed to the man-made pleasure and leisure business.

7. The pupils may write a piece of work on 'My Holiday' focussing on the naturally occurring environment.

8. Alternatively they may write a comparative piece of work looking at the relative merits and demerits of holidays in naturally occurring surroundings or in a man-made environment.

9. Less able pupils can make a drawing of a holiday or day out in natural surroundings if their literacy ability is insufficient to undertake creative writing.

NOW AND THEN, HERE AND THERE

The objectives of this lesson are to test and increase the pupils' general knowledge in the humanities.

1. Divide the group into three or four teams of equal size and if possible roughly equal ability.

2. Appoint a team leader for each team.

3. Explain to the pupils that they are going to take part in a team quiz. Some of the questions will be for a particular team, others will be open to anyone to answer.

4. If a team are unable to answer their set question, another team may do so.

5. In this way a points total will accrue to each team, and there will be ongoing competition to find correct answers.

6. The teacher sets all of the questions and decides whether they are open to all or offered to a specific team. The teacher is also the final arbiter when answers are given.

7. The questions will vary depending on the age and ability of the pupils, and possibly even dependent on their recent or current courses of study.

8. The theme of the questions reflects a broad historical and geographic field ('Now and then, here and there'). They may range from the very simple 'Who is the Prime Minister of Great Britain?', to the more complicated 'Name five types of clouds'.

9. The crucial thing about the questions is that the teacher must know the answer! Ideally reference books may be used, but if this is impractical all teachers will have a basic body of knowledge on which to draw.

10. It is, of course, possible to widen the scope of the questions to take in natural history, religious knowledge or any other curriculum area as desired. This may then develop into a genuine 'trivia' quiz with which the pupils may be more familiar.

Lesson Completion Chart

LESSON	CLASS	DATE

NOTES

LESSON	CLASS	DATE

NOTES

LESSON	CLASS	DATE

NOTES

LESSON	CLASS	DATE

NOTES

LESSON	CLASS	DATE

NOTES

LESSON	CLASS	DATE

NOTES

LESSON	CLASS	DATE

NOTES

LESSON	CLASS	DATE

NOTES

LESSON	CLASS	DATE

NOTES

LESSON	CLASS	DATE

NOTES

LESSON	CLASS	DATE

NOTES

LESSON	CLASS	DATE

NOTES

LESSON	CLASS	DATE

NOTES

LESSON	CLASS	DATE

NOTES

LESSON	CLASS	DATE

NOTES

LESSON	CLASS	DATE

NOTES

LESSON	CLASS	DATE

NOTES

LESSON	CLASS	DATE

NOTES

LESSON	CLASS	DATE

NOTES

LESSON	CLASS	DATE

NOTES

LESSON	CLASS	DATE

NOTES

LESSON	CLASS	DATE

NOTES

LESSON	CLASS	DATE

NOTES

LESSON	CLASS	DATE

NOTES

1

2

3

4

4

5

6

6

Venice
in Watercolour

Joe Francis Dowden

SEARCH PRESS

First published in Great Britain 2011

Search Press Limited
Wellwood, North Farm Road,
Tunbridge Wells, Kent TN2 3DR

Photographs by Roddy Paine and Gavin Sawyer at Roddy Paine Photographic Studios, and Debbie Patterson at Search Press Studios

ISBN: 978-1-84448-491-1

Suppliers
If you have any difficulty obtaining any of the materials and equipment mentioned in this book, please visit the Search Press website: www.searchpress.com

Publisher's note
All the step-by-step photographs in this book feature the author, Joe Francis Dowden, demonstrating watercolour painting techniques. No models have been used.

You are invited to visit the author's website at www.joedowden.com

Please note that when removing the perforated sheets of tracing paper from the book, score them first, then carefully pull out each sheet.

Printed in China

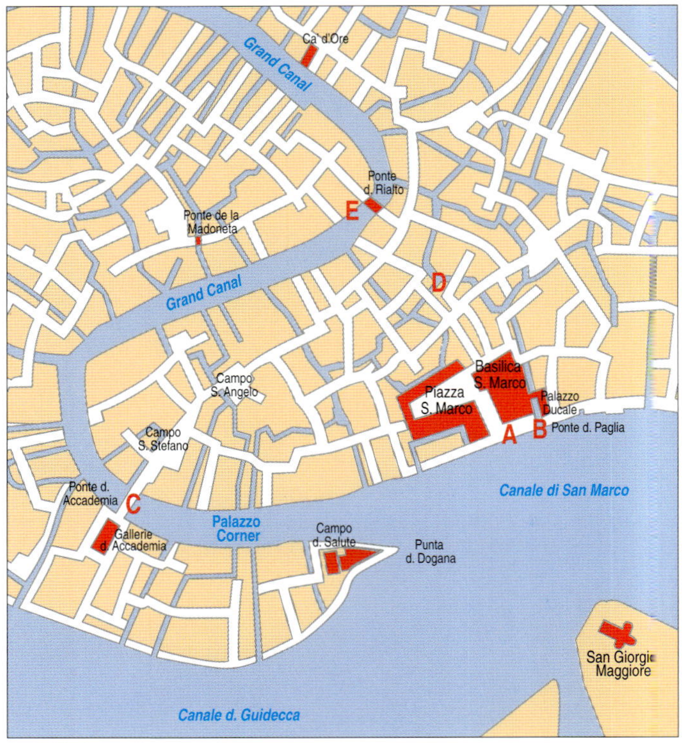

Map of Venice with project sites marked

This map of Venice shows the sites of the five step-by-step projects in this book marked in red: **A** *Gondolas,* **B** *Venetian Skyline,* **C** *The Grand Canal,* **D** *The Heart of Venice and* **E** *Rialto Bridge.*

Page 1

The Gondolier Returns

40 x 30cm (15¾ x 11¾in)

Late evening, and I viewed this scene from below the Accademia Bridge on the south bank of the Grand Canal looking east. Tone is more important than colour, and is used here to create both subtle and powerful contrasts. The grey sky projects the architecture by having been painted around it and leaving light for buildings. First a pale, watery brown wash was applied to everything, leaving just a few whites here and there. When this was thoroughly dry, the sky area was painted with a grey mix. After two layers of colour, this left three layers of tone: light, white and grey sky. The water was painted in three layers: a darker brown layer based on raw sienna to reflect the buildings; a blue layer, leaving the light reflected area of the left-hand buildings but with a few dragged ripples; and a dark layer for the darker ripples. The gondolier and his boat were masked and finished at the end.

Opposite

Venetian Gold

45 x 30cm (17¾ x 11¾in)

I observed this view from the Rialto Bridge one October evening, looking down the canal towards San Marco. Raw sienna, burnt sienna, quinacridone gold, Naples yellow, quinacridone magenta, French ultramarine, cobalt blue and Payne's gray were used to paint it. The buildings were placed using wet washes and the colours were allowed to mix freely on the paper to achieve a general sense of the buildings rather than an accurate depiction. The bottoms of the buildings were left broken up and ragged to give the illusion of detail at canal level. When dry, smaller flat brushes were used to drag vertical darks down for shadow, and a tiny flat brush was used to place windows, always with a single stroke. Some windows are simply squares of underlying colour left behind in the overlying wash. The final darks consisted of the boats and posts painted with Payne's gray or neutral tint.

Contents

Introduction

TRACING 1

There are so many lovely places to see on the earth, but most of us never get the chance to visit more than a small fraction of them. However, with these *Ready to Paint* books, you can visit a growing list of destinations simply by painting them. The medium I have used is watercolour but there is no reason why you shouldn't try painting them in any medium you choose.

I have picked for you the most attractive views of Venice I could find, in the best possible lighting conditions. If you wish to visit them yourself, the map on page 2 will show you where they are. You could use the tracings to draw the scene first before going there and painting it on site. You could also paint the first washes to get you started so you won't have to wait for them to dry. A few years ago I drew the French town of Rocomadour on a May morning, but didn't have time to paint it before the early morning light had changed to harsh mid-day sun. So in November I returned with the original drawing and did the painting during the morning.

This book, in common with the other titles in this series, aims to make it easier for you to achieve a successful painting and to improve your technique. It allows you to develop your painting without being restricted by the quality of your initial drawing – most of us want to get on and paint, and my job is to guide you through each project, step by step.

All of the projects in the book measure 41.5 x 29.5cm (16½ x 11¾in), though you could scale the tracings up or down to get different sizes. Each project, and the painting opposite, is accompanied by a pull-out tracing at the front of the book, which can be transferred easily to your watercolour paper by following the instructions on page 9.

Remember to take the time at the start of each project to mix plenty of colour. If you don't have exactly the same colours as those I have used, don't panic, and simply use similar colours instead. Always have more than enough mixed colour to hand, as well as plenty of clean water, a sharp pencil and a well-pointing brush. Apply colour generously, then leave it alone. Let it dry and add more colour at the next step. Do not overwork any stage of your painting.

Keep your painting area clear and free of clutter so that you can swivel your painting around and work at it from any angle. Turn your painting to suit the natural sweep of your hand. You can also tip it in any direction to allow the paint to flow.

I am interested in helping you develop as an artist, no matter what your level is. My dad taught me to paint and my mum always encouraged me in whatever I did, so together they taught me a lot. Not many painters have this advantage in life, so it's my privilege to pass it on to you.

Happy painting!

Gondola

30 x 42cm (11¾ x 16½in)

This is the Madoneta Canal, looking south from Ponte de la Madoneta, Calle de la Madoneta, San Polo. The key to this painting is not colour, but tone. Having masked out the gondola and the gondolier completely, along with some of the finer details that I wanted to leave until the end, I started the painting with pale, grey washes of blues, violets and browns. Once these were dry, I started building the painting in layers of colour, one area at a time. As the tones were built up, the painting got progressively stronger. Colour can be built up in many layers, as long as each individual layer is not overworked and is left to dry totally.

The water was painted in two layers. I started with a very deep blackish blue to the right of the gondola then, when this was completely dry, I mixed a dark green, an intense dark mix of Paynes gray and a turquoise. I applied the paint very fast and wet, leaving the lighter undercoat for the ripples at the front of the boat. When dry, I removed the masking and painted the boats and details. I got away with using some very bright colours in this painting because they were balanced by the intense darks and strong greys.

Materials

It is amazing what you can do with just a few art materials. I continue to experiment, and recommend that you do the same. I am always delighted to find some new brush or tool that gives a particular effect, like the water sparkles in *Gondolas*, achieved by stippling on masking fluid with a cheap, hog-hair brush. It isn't simply about what works best, either. When you use different materials it can change your approach and refresh and invigorate your work. Mine is not necessarily a big palette, just a changeable one. Be guided by the advice below, but don't stick to it too rigidly, and your painting will be all the better for it.

Paints

Venice is peppered with rich colours. At one time it was the lapis lazuli and yellow gold leaf on the palace façades of the fabulously rich. Nowadays, blue paint is cheap, but some of the palaces are a shadow of their former selves. However, look into the Venetian shadows for rich reds, streaks of ochre, deep tertiaries of turquoise and emerald in the water, violet on the shaded walls of buildings, and bright colours dotted like distant echoes of an opulent past. If you don't have all the colours I have used in the projects you can innovate and use other colours. Excellent results can also be obtained by using a palette with only the following colours: French ultramarine, cobalt blue, phthalo blue, burnt sienna, quinacridone magenta, cadmium lemon and Payne's gray.

You can use strong colours as long as you use dense dark tone in the same painting. My Venice covers the full range of tone and colour, so enjoy using your materials and look for other interpretations of my images.

Paper

Choice of paper is very important and a good-quality watercolour paper makes a difference to your finished painting. Colours will look more vibrant and you will find it easier to get good results.

Watercolour paper comes in three types of surface: hot pressed (HP), which has a smooth surface; NOT (or not hot pressed, otherwise known as cold pressed) and rough, both of which have a rough surface. The best quality watercolour papers are made of cotton, linen or both, and are either handmade or mould-made using a cylinder mould machine. Size has been added either internally, being mixed in with the furnish, or externally by soaking – 'tub sized'.

In all the projects in this book I have used Arches Aquarelle 300gsm (140lb) rough, though you can, of course, use any good-quality rough or NOT paper of a similar weight. This is a mould-made, cotton-fibre, tub-sized mellow white paper. It will not go yellow, has a very tough surface, and shows colour very brightly. It also does not rip when masked and is immensely strong and reliable. I recommend stretching the paper beforehand by soaking it and fixing it to a board while wet. This makes it as tight as a drum skin when dry and prevents it from buckling. I either use gummed tape wetted with a sponge to stick it down, or staple with light- to medium-duty 4mm (¼in) staples. I remove them afterwards with a tack lifter and a self-grip wrench.

Brushes, pens and colour shapers

My main brushes are mid-sized sables, nos 6 to 8, and detail sables of sizes 2 to 4. I also have brushes that I use for specific jobs.

4cm (1½in) hake: this is a large flat brush made of goat hair or 'hake', now the generic name for this type of flat brush. It is useful for applying washes, especially when putting another wash over a dried wash (glazing).

Sable round brushes, nos 2–4, 6–8 and 12: though round, these form a good point when wet, and are extremely controllable. You can clean a sable brush and use it for another colour much faster than a synthetic brush. The larger round brushes are useful for washes where more control is needed, such as painting a sky around buildings.

Squirrel mop brush: I sometimes use this instead of a no. 12 round when looser work is desired.

Older brushes: useful for mixing colour on the palette; use your best brushes for painting only.

Stiff-bristle flat brush: useful for scrubbing out colour or 'lifting'.

Flat brushes, 4cm (1½in) and 3–6mm (¼in): sable or synthetic; a large and a small flat brush are useful for painting the flat sides of buildings down from the straight-edged roof line. For painting details, the smaller the brush the better.

Fan blender: the one I use is a mongoose fan. This is probably the best material for a fan blender because the fibres are soft but firm and splay out well without tending to gather. I use this brush for blending wet colours together to create smooth effects in water.

Indian ink pen (dip pen): this is a separate pen nib pushed into the end of a shaft or pen handle. I use it for accurate masking using liquid masking fluid.

Ruling pen: this type of pen consists of a pair of dividers and a metal screw wheel that allows you to finely adjust the thickness of line. It can be used to apply fine lines of masking fluid.

Colour shaper: This is a shaft with a neoprene head instead of fibres. Designed for pastel painters, it is a useful applicator for masking fluid.

Just some of the brushes I have used in the projects in this book. Don't worry if you don't have all of those listed here – different-sized brushes will give similar results, and you can even get by with just one well-pointed sable.

Other materials

Masking fluid can be used either protectively or constructively. Protective masking involves covering white or light areas to paint later. This allows you to paint the surrounding image without having to worry about painting around the masked object – you can paint straight across it and it will appear as a neat, unpainted shape when you take off the masking fluid. Constructive masking involves using the inherent qualities of masking fluid to produce beautiful texture and detail using special techniques, for example the sparkles in *Gondolas* or the brickwork in *The Heart of Venice*.

Applying a tiny amount of **gum arabic** before laying paint into water reflections can slow blending, allowing many soft-focus colours to remain separate and give a super wet look to reflections.

Masking tape is used to define the outer edge of your painting, allowing you to paint over it and still give a crisp edge to your work. It is also useful for masking off larger areas to achieve clean, straight lines.

A **large bucket and two or three jars** for holding water while painting – essential for adding water to your mixes and for cleaning your brush when changing from one colour to another.

Use **paper towel** for 'lifting' and cleaning up odd spills and splashes of paint.

I don't use a conventional palette for mixing my colours instead I use a collection of **old white china plates** – one for each of my mixes. This allows me to mix up large quantities of colour prior to starting to paint.

Viewing my painting through a **mirror** reverses the image. This helps me to see my painting afresh, and spot mistakes early so I can correct them before the painting is complete.

A **grade B pencil** is good for making the initial drawing. You may also need an **eraser** for correcting mistakes, and a **pencil sharpener**.

It is all right to use a **ruler** sometimes for straight lines, and you can also trust your eye and work freehand. Both are valid and there really is no rule. It is surprising how much charm a few wandering wavy lines can add to your image. I use both methods.

Transferring the image

For each project, use a piece of watercolour paper that is larger than your finished painting and then trim it to size once your painting is complete. Stretch the paper and fix it to your board (see page 6), then transfer the image. Tracings are provided at the front of this book for all the demonstration paintings, together with an additional tracing for the painting shown on page 5. Follow the steps below to transfer the drawings on to your watercolour paper. You can reuse each tracing several times, so you could use the same basic image to produce two quite different paintings.

1 Place the tracing face down. Trace over the lines on the back using a B-grade pencil. You will be able to reuse this tracing several times without repeating this step.

2 Tape a sheet of watercolour paper to a board and place the tracing, face up, on top. Now tape down the tracing. Draw carefully and firmly over the lines of the tracing again.

3 As you work, lift up the tracing every now and then to see how the transfer of the image is going. Strengthen the image on the paper if necessary.

Once the image has been transferred, lay masking tape along each edge of the drawing (see page 6). This will give a clean, crisp edge to your finished painting.

Gondolas

TRACING 2

It was mid-afternoon, and I viewed this scene from Molo San Marco, along the shoreline of the Lagoon in front of the Palazzo Ducale (Doge's Palace), looking towards the island of San Giorgio Maggiore. The viewpoint is more or less in front of the palace itself.

Even if you have never been to this place, you may have seen it many times, but how do you paint it? Notice the strong tones and the sparkles masked out at the outset. This scene is easier to paint than it looks. Mix plenty of colour, take it one step at a time and be confident with your brushwork.

You will need

Paper: 55 x 36cm (21¾ x 14¼in), 300gsm (140lb) Arches rough watercolour paper

Colours: quinacridone red, quinacridone magenta, Winsor violet, French ultramarine, cobalt blue, cyan (or phthalo) blue, cerulean blue, phthalo green, Naples yellow, burnt sienna, indigo, Payne's gray

Brushes: 3 sable rounds (nos 8, 6 and 3)

Cheap hog-hair brush, colour shaper, Indian ink pen and masking fluid

Small flat brush and an eraser

Paper towel

1 Mask out the 'sparkles' on the water by dabbing on the masking fluid with the tip of a cheap, stiff brush.

2 Change to a colour shaper and mask out the ropes and thin whites, in other words anything that is difficult to paint around loosely. For very fine lines, use an Indian ink pen to apply the masking fluid.

3 Using the no. 8 round, put a wash of clean water over the sky area; there is no need to go round the edges of the buildings. While it is still wet, put in the grey sky tone of quinacridone magenta, cobalt blue and burnt sienna, starting on the left-hand side of the painting. Take the colour down to just below the bottom of the sky area.

4 While it is still wet, bring a little more quinacridone magenta into the mix for the lower part of the sky, and a little more blue at the top. Add in more water as you move to the right of the picture so that the colour fades out. Allow the sky to dry thoroughly before applying the washes for the water.

5 Working wet on dry, lay on a blue wash of cyan blue mixed with cobalt blue. Work around the boats. Make the mix more watery as you drag the colour across to the right and down towards the bottom of the picture. To achieve the sparkly water on the right, hold the brush flat against the paper and drag it across.

6 Keeping it wet, lay on a strong mix of phthalo green, cyan blue and burnt sienna for the lower area of water (it will go paler as it dries). Work quickly, in broad, horizontal strokes.

7 Blend the water colour with the turquoise above, going carefully around the shapes of the boats. Bring in a little quinacridone magenta on the right of the picture to make the colour more violet. Avoid a smooth wash – vary it to mimic the ripples on the surface of the water.

8 Still keeping it wet, continue to strengthen the water colour. Put in the deep undertones of the surface ripples using a stronger version of the same mix. When you have finished, tilt the board up at a slight angle and allow the paint to dry.

9 When the water is completely dry, lay a sweep of light blue-grey over the background buildings, consisting of cerulean blue, burnt sienna and a little quinacridone magenta.

10 When the grey wash has dried, change to a no. 6 brush with a good point, make a stronger wash of the same mix and start to put in the detail. Vary the mix slightly as you work, for example drop in a little more quinacridone magenta here and there to hint at brickwork. Use a no. 3 brush for the finer detail, such as windows. Gradually build up the tone to contrast with the water, but keep it light enough to push the buildings into the background.

11 With the point of the no. 3 brush, put in the distant boats and poles on the right using a reddish-grey mix of cerulean blue, burnt sienna and quinacridone magenta. Bleed in from the sides some French ultramarine for the darker parts of the boat, and use the same colour for the pontoons. Put a little more dark into the background where required.

12 Use the no. 6 brush and a mix of cyan blue with a little indigo and quinacridone magenta to put in the first boat on the right. Change to pure cyan blue and lay it over the back part of the boat, leaving a few whites. Continue putting the same blue on all the boats, working from right to left. Run in some phthalo green here and there to vary the colour a little.

13 When dry, add a little more indigo to the mix and work your way across the painting again, from right to left, putting in the mid-tone shadow. Switch to the no. 3 brush where more control is required. Don't be afraid to use strong colours – they will dry a little lighter.

14 Make a darker blue mix by adding more indigo and a little Winsor violet, and add another layer of dark folds, leaving some folds in the previous layer unpainted. Use a stronger mix for the most intense darks. For detail, refer to the finished painting.

15 Put in the greys using Payne's gray mixed with a little of the blue. Work from right to left, as before. Add water to the mix to vary the tone if required.

16 Strengthen the greys where needed and gradually build up the tones. Paint carefully around the white stripes on the sides of the boats with the no. 3 brush. These stripes show as the grey from the previous wash and are not to be confused with the white lines masked at the outset.

17 For the mooring poles, use a mix of cerulean blue and burnt sienna and a clean no. 3 brush. Wet the first pole, lay the colour down the shaded side and allow it to spread across to the other. While it is still wet, darken the pole along its darkest edge. Notice that the poles are slightly wider at the top.

18 Put in the rest of the poles. Tonally, the poles should have an almost 'ghostly' appearance, but be strong enough to stand out from the background buildings. The smaller poles can be painted using a single colour. Scan over the painting and put in the rowlocks (forcola) and any remaining detailing on the boats using a range of your greys and darks.

19 Using the tip of the no. 3 brush, put in the tiny red patches on the boats using quinacridone red.

20 Using a blue-green mix of burnt sienna, cyan blue and phthalo green and the no. 3 brush, put in the harder wave patterns in the background. On the right, drag the flat side of the brush from side to side to get a sparkling effect, then put in some very faint marks in the mid-ground and left using cyan blue.

21 Come further into the foreground and make the marks more pronounced. Change to the no. 6 brush and use the cyan mixed with the blue-green mix of the previous step together with Naples yellow. Mix plenty of colour.

22 Emphasise the marks more as you work forwards, and develop them into the reflection under one of the boats. Add some Payne's gray just underneath the boat and blend it downwards into the reflection. Change to the no. 3 brush if required.

23 Bring the colour across the painting to the next boat using the yellowy-green mix of burnt sienna, cyan blue, phthalo green and Naples yellow. Put the dark green mix of burnt sienna, cyan blue and phthalo green under the boat and blend it in. Use either the no. 3 or the no. 6 brush, depending on the size of brushstroke required.

24 Put in the reflection of the pole using the no. 3 brush and the dark green mix, and the occasional small, circular ripple. Work loosely using plenty of colour. The ripples do not have to be exactly the same shapes as in the original painting.

25 Working quickly, continue across to the next boat, painting in the reflections using the yellowy-green and dark green mixes (see step 23). Darken the reflections with Payne's gray where required, and put in the darker lines connecting adjacent reflections using the no. 3 round brush.

26 Put a very dark reflection under the boat on the far right.

27 Align a piece of masking tape along the edge of the blue fabric and darken the boat up to this edge. The tape preserves the contrasting edge of the lighter fabric tone whichever way you brush. This is a useful way to preserve edges.

28 Darken the areas under the boats using a very dark mix. Keep the colours strong and work wet into wet.

29 For the 'sparkles', use a damp flat brush to rub across the masked highlights using up-and-down movements to lift blurred vertical highlights, then dab with a piece of paper towel. When completely dry, remove the masking fluid.

30 Remove all the remaining masking fluid, revealing the whites underneath. You can use an eraser to rub off any stubborn patches of masking fluid.

31 Add some pale grey to the ropes. Put in the light reflections on the shiny side of the boats using a pale green mix of blue and Naples yellow. Gloss over them with water to blend them in. Use the same pale green mix to put a hint of lighter reflections here and there in the water.

Venetian Skyline

I came across this view one evening. I was looking south-west from the top of the Ponte de la Pagia, which crosses the Rio de la Canonica Canal, bordering the Palazzo Ducale (Doge's Palace).

Don't be intimidated by all the people. Most are painted with just a few brushstrokes, some with a single stroke, and there are so many that together they will look fine no matter what you do. Focus on what they are doing rather than what they look like. If they are carrying a bag, for example, paint them leaning; if they are with a child, single brushstrokes for the arms holding hands will tell the story. Keep the heads small and directly above the load-bearing heel. Bodies should be approximately seven and a half times as long as heads for men and six and a half times as long for women.

This painting is unified with a mix of cerulean blue, burnt sienna and quinacridone magenta, which I have used throughout.

You will need

Paper: 55 x 36cm (21¾ x 14¼in), 300gsm (140lb) Arches rough watercolour paper

Colours: quinacridone magenta, French ultramarine, cerulean blue, Naples yellow, raw sienna, burnt sienna and Payne's gray

Brushes: 2 sable rounds (nos 7 and 3), large flat brush

Indian ink pen and masking fluid

Masking tape

Ruler

Tip

Spend time mixing up the colours you will need before starting to paint, using the finished painting for guidance. Test them out on a spare piece of watercolour paper. When you have got the colour you want, mix up a large quantity of it – muddy colours result from not mixing enough colour for a wash, and then going over and over it with weak colour to no real effect.

Another cause of muddy colour is simply not trusting in your washes, and overworking them while they are wet. Put them down and leave them alone. You can paint as many overlying washes as you like, as long as the previous ones are completely dry.

1 Paint masking fluid on to the lamps using an Indian ink pen. Allow it to dry.

2 Using a large flat brush, lay a wash of clean water over the whole picture.

3 Place the board at a slight angle so that the colour runs down, then use a no. 7 round brush to lay on a watery glaze of Naples yellow, burnt sienna and cerulean blue. Add quinacridone magenta to the mix as you get closer to the buildings.

Tip

Try to look at your picture in terms of tone only, and paint the shapes made by the different tones. This will require careful observation.

4 Work your way over the whole of the sky area, building up the colour while retaining the light. Take the colour down towards the ground area, adding some cerulean blue to the mix to achieve a deeper tone over the building area.

5 Using a mix of raw sienna, burnt sienna and quinacridone magenta, build up the colours at the bottom of the picture. If the initial water glaze has started to dry, wet it again. Keep the central ground area paler.

Tip

Continue painting on the base washes, and the colours will get stronger and stronger; the more colour you can get on to your painting in the early stages the better.

6 Darken the ground by adding some cerulean blue and burnt sienna. Leave the central area lighter. Allow the painting to dry.

7 Raise the board a little higher so that the colour flows downwards. Make two very wet mixes – one of burnt sienna, Naples yellow and quinacridone magenta for the lighter cloud shapes, and one of burnt sienna, cerulean blue and quinacridone magenta for the darker cloud shadows. Lay on the colours in horizontal strokes.

8 Take the wet colour down over the buildings, bringing in more blue as you move downwards. Allow a dark edge to form where the ground meets the water. The colours may look very strong at this stage, but they will dry lighter. Hold the painting vertically to encourage the colours to run downwards if necessary. Leave to dry thoroughly, allowing the granulation to develop.

Tip

Build up your painting in layers, allowing each layer to dry thoroughly before applying the next, otherwise successive layers will travel through to the underlying paint and muddy it.

9 Lay a piece of masking tape diagonally across the lower right-hand corner to mask off the area of paving. Using the burnt sienna, cerulean blue and quinacridone magenta mix, put in horizontal sweeps of colour across the ground area. Work quickly to avoid the paint drying out and take the colour right up to the edge of the water, including the jetties. Retain the light patch in the middle of the picture, going down to a slightly smaller brush to work round the brighter areas if necessary. The aim is to achieve the effect of glinting sunlight.

10 When the ground has dried thoroughly, use a light, grey-blue mix of burnt sienna, cerulean blue and quinacridone magenta to put on the next layer – the buildings. Use a well-pointed no. 7 brush, and keep the paint moving – make sure you mix plenty of colour before you start so that you don't run out. Start by painting the domes, and change to a no. 3 brush for the finer detail. Leave tiny gaps for light in the delicate dome-top structures.

11 Add neat burnt sienna to the lower parts of the wash, then go back to the original mix to define the steps and the structures on the top of the tall building and the column on the right. Allow to dry.

12 Make up a stronger version of the blue-grey mix and start putting on the darker layers. Starting with the dome, use the tip of the no. 3 brush to wet the top, then darken the sides. Colour will run into the wet area.

13 Continue putting in the darker detailing on the buildings. Refer closely to the finished painting, and paint what you see. Use a slightly warmer mix for the roofs, and for each window use a single brushstroke applied with the tip of the brush.

14 Mask along the outer edge of the near shore with masking tape. Use the no. 7 brush to put in the darker areas on the ground. Use the same mix as that used for the buildings. Start with the dark area on the left and move right, changing to a smaller brush to achieve finer brushstrokes in the lighter areas.

15 Go back and strengthen the dark area to the left by adding French ultramarine and burnt sienna. Use the finer brush to darken the ground on the right using thinner lines. Remove the masking tape.

16 Mix some French ultramarine and burnt sienna in a dark mix and a lighter, rich brown variant. Wet the foliage area and add the colour, letting it spread through the wet area without painting it right to the edge of the trees. As you approach the edge of the foliage, use a warmer brown mix with less French ultramarine.

17 Working further along to the right, use a very dark mix of French ultramarine and burnt sienna to add in the dark wooden poles and the hut in the centre of the painting. Also, start to map in the crowd in the background. Leave plenty of lights to suggest the spaces between people.

18 Bring the crowd forward and suggest individual figures with downward strokes. Consult the finished painting for the general feel rather than accuracy.

Tip

When suggesting people in the background, keep the heads small for a more realistic effect.

19 Put in a strip of masking tape to mark the ends of the jetties, and start to paint them in with a strong, dark mix of French ultramarine and burnt sienna. For the diagonals, keep a constant angle throughout. Use a ruler if you prefer.

20 Put in the vertical poles along the jetties. Avoid making them too regular – vary their length and thickness, and place them at slightly different angles.

21 Complete the darks, putting in the end of each boat using a single, curved brushstroke. Strengthen the blacks where necessary. Remove the masking tape and use a damp brush to lift out any excess paint that has bled underneath.

22 Remove the masking tape you put in place in step 9. Finish the paving on the right using the no. 7 brush, laying on a mix of burnt sienna, cerulean blue and quinacridone magenta in broad, diagonal brushstrokes. Lay on the shadows across the paving using a darker version of the same mix.

23 Put in the group of people on the left, and add a little Naples yellow to a reddish-grey mix of burnt sienna, cerulean blue and quinacridone magenta to put in the faces of the four figures in the foreground.

24 Returning to the very dark mix of French ultramarine and burnt sienna, paint in the main figures, following the finished painting closely. Add some Payne's gray to the mix for more depth of colour. Use plenty of strong colour but keep the brushstrokes slender.

26 Map in some blues, reds and purples on the right of the picture where there is a market stall just in view. This does not need to be defined too closely.

Tip

When painting foreground figures, avoid adding too much detail. Decide where the edges of the figure are and keep within them. Avoid curves – work in straight lines. Children are defined only by their size and what they are wearing.

25 Put in the rest of the figures in the middle and background. Close up some of the spaces in the background crowd to achieve the effect of a mass of people. Notice the fine limbs, which taper to a point.

28 Paint in the lamp posts using Payne's gray. For the stone base of the lamp posts, use a mix of cerulean blue, burnt sienna and quinacridone magenta.

27 Darken the column on the right and the building behind it to bring them forward using the buildings mix of cerulean blue, burnt sienna and quinacridone magenta. Lay the colour over the whole surface using broad brushstrokes, fading it out towards the base. Use the tip of the brush to strengthen the structures on the top of the column and the building and to put a strong black shadow down the right-hand side of the column. Dampen the left-hand edge of the shadow and let the colour bleed across.

Tip

Reinstate any pencil outlines that have become lost by laying the tracing back over the painting and transferring the relevant parts of the drawing.

29 Strengthen the dark waterline at the base of the buildings, place further dark accents here and there, and add some horizontal marks in the water using a mix of French ultramarine and burnt sienna. With burnt sienna and cerulean blue, put in the awning that is just visible on the left. Make a large quantity of a blue version of the mix using cerulean blue, quinacridone magenta and burnt sienna, then put in the shadows. Use a ruler to make sure they are straight and all pointing towards the sun. To help you do this, make a pencil dot in the distant buildings above the crowd, just to the left of the lamp, and line up the ruler on this mark for all the shadows.

Tip

To make your shadows realistic, make sure you locate the light source accurately and ensure all the shadows point towards it. Here, the light source (the sun) is just right of centre top.

30 Add the finishing touches to your painting. Place tiny touches of Naples yellow mixed with a little quinacridone magenta here and there, for example on the hats of the group of gondoliers to the left. With the tip of the brush, paint on the cracks in the paving on the right using a very dark mix of French ultramarine and burnt sienna, and continue with some thin, black lines on the main walkway to suggest paving slabs. On the left, strengthen the darks still further by dry brushing in the very dark mix.

31 Rub off the masking fluid, then paint the lamps using burnt sienna and the no. 3 brush. Leave the lamp tops white, then paint them in with Payne's gray, leaving thin white lines along some of the edges to make them shine (see the finished painting). Put in the vertical black edges of the glass casing on the lamps, then complete the painting by dry brushing some brown on to the surface of the water using the no. 3 brush.

The Grand Canal

TRACING 4

This view, which I observed late one afternoon, is from the Accademia Bridge, looking east down the Grand Canal towards its confluence with the Lagoon.

Get the simple tonal washes down at the outset and the rest of the painting will follow through in logical stages. The painting is all about simple blocks of contrasting tone. The sky, for example, reveals the domes, rising like icebergs behind the dark edifices along the canal. The sunshine is reflected off the light façades on the left. This painting is all about light against dark, dark against light. Apply this to all your work to give it impact.

You will need

Paper: 55 x 36cm (21¾ x 14¼in), 300gsm (140lb) Arches rough watercolour paper

Colours: cadmium lemon, quinacridone magenta, French ultramarine, cobalt blue, phthalo blue, cerulean blue, cobalt turquoise light, phthalo green, Naples yellow, yellow ochre, burnt sienna, Payne's gray

Brushes: 3 sable rounds (nos 12, 6 and 3), fan blender, 4cm (1½in) hake (or flat brush), small flat brush

Colour shaper, Indian ink pen and masking fluid

Masking tape

Paper towel

1 Paint masking fluid on to the domes, chimneys, poles, flags, the distant gondolas and any other small shapes you wish to paint around. Use an Indian ink pen for applying the masking fluid to smaller shapes, and a colour shaper for larger ones.

2 When the masking fluid is dry, glaze the sky with water. Use a no. 12 round brush, and take the water down to the roof line, painting carefully around the buildings. While the glaze is still wet, lay on a glaze of quinacridone magenta using horizontal brushstrokes, starting at the roof line and taking the colour halfway up the sky area.

3 Use a fan brush to blend the colour upwards, then smooth out the colour with the no. 12 brush.

4 Apply a band of yellow ochre above the red, then smooth and blend the two colours together. Re-wet the top part of the sky, if necessary, and put in a band of phthalo blue, fading it towards the left. Blend all three colours together with the fan brush.

5 Tilt the board so that the colour runs from the bottom to the top, and neaten the colour around the roof line using a no. 6 brush. Touch in a little cobalt blue along the horizon to darken it, and let the colour spread upwards. Allow the paint to dry.

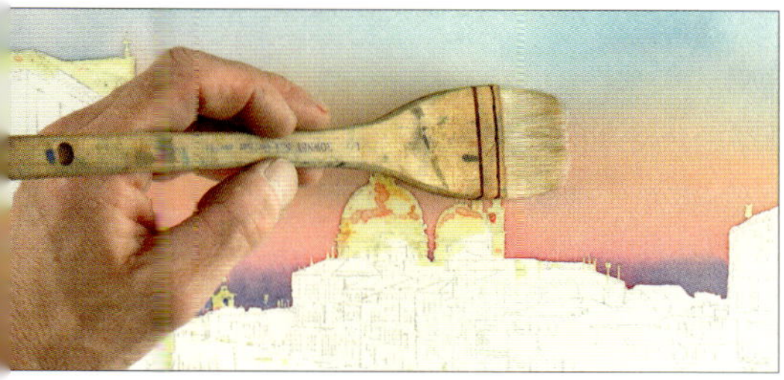

6 For the second layer, first dampen the sky with a 4cm (1½in) hake or flat brush to get the water on quickly (otherwise the first layer may lift).

7 Lay phthalo blue on to the top of the sky with the no. 12 brush. Build up a strong layer of blue, as it will dry paler.

8 Take the phthalo blue down to the roof line, then darken the horizon further using French ultramarine. Blend the dark blue into the rest of the sky using the fan brush. Tip the board so that the paint runs upwards.

Tip

When allowing a wash to dry, carefully lift the masking tape at the edge of the picture to prevent colour from gathering beneath it and then seeping back to spoil your painting.

9 As the sky dries, a slight gathering of pigment around the domes will make them stand out more against the sky. When it is completely dry, wet the canal in vertical brushstrokes to pick up the undercurrent of vertical reflections, then lay in strong, vertical stripes of burnt sienna using the no. 12 brush.

10 Mix a little yellow ochre with the burnt sienna and take the colour right up to the shoreline on the left. Leave a few soft vertical lights. Add a little quinacridone magenta here and there. Change to a smaller brush and put in the distant section of water using French ultramarine.

11 Bring the blue forward and blend it in with the orange. Change back to the no. 12 brush and strengthen the orange colour, particularly where it is close to the buildings in the foreground. Blend all the colours seamlessly.

12 With a clean brush, put in strong, vertical stripes of phthalo blue, taking the colour right up to the buildings in the background. Blend the colours together with the fan brush, as before. Keep it wet for the next stage.

13 Continue to build up colour. Mix a blackish blue by adding Payne's gray to phthalo blue and put in the darks under the buildings in the far distance. Drag the colour down and blend it into the rest of the water.

14 Darken the shaded areas on the left, then take the fan brush with a little blue on it and blend the paint, retaining subtle areas of light and dark. Allow to dry.

15 Mix a green using Naples yellow, phthalo blue and a little quinacridone magenta, and lightly paint in the distant parkland. Begin with the intense darks at the base, then add a little more Naples yellow to create patches of light.

16 Carefully remove the masking fluid from the domes by rubbing one corner gently and peeling it off with your fingers. Using a well-pointed, no. 3 brush, paint each dome with water, then add a mix of cerulean blue and burnt sienna to the left-hand side. Allow the colour to bleed across to the right. While still wet, add a little more colour on the left and at the base of the dome.

17 Working wet into wet, lay more shadow colour on the left-hand side of the largest dome. Let it dry. Notice the neat darkening of the definition line edging the dome caused by pigment gathering along the overlap with the sky wash. Dry brush on more colour to add texture, and touch in the small tower on top of the main dome. Lay Naples yellow over the tops of the buildings below the domes, followed by grey to make cream. Put some backlighting on the smaller dome.

18 Continue to build up the details on the domes using dark greys. Avoid overworking the windows, and keep them small. Build up the darks in two or three layers using wet on dry, and strengthen the shadows.

19 While the domes are drying, mix a red using yellow ochre, burnt sienna and a little quinacridone magenta and put in the roofs with the no. 3 brush.

20 Put in the façades using various mixes of quinacridone magenta, cerulean blue, burnt sienna and a little Naples yellow. Start on the left and work your way along using vertical brushstrokes. Allow to dry.

21 Complete the lower part of the domes using a light grey mix of cobalt blue and burnt sienna. Start to put the windows, shadows and detailing on to the buildings, beginning on the left with a dark red mix of quinacridone magenta, French ultramarine and burnt sienna.

22 Work your way across the painting, referring closely to the finished piece. For the darker tones, use a mix of cerulean blue, French ultramarine and burnt sienna. Leave lights for the window apertures. When dry, use a dark mix of burnt sienna and French ultramarine to paint the darker window apertures, all dark details and the shadows along the lower parts of the buildings. The light sides of the buildings are painted using a pale version of the roof colour – yellow ochre, burnt sienna and a little quinacridone magenta.

23 Brush some dark reds on to the roofs using wet on dry, then put in the dark green foliage visible behind the buildings using phthalo blue mixed with a little burnt sienna.

24 Move to the foreground buildings on the left, and lay a pale mix of Naples yellow on to the first building on the right using a no. 6 brush. Leave a few loose lights to hint at windows.

25 Mask the edges of the projecting roof using masking tape and paint in the roof using the same red as before (yellow ochre, burnt sienna and a little quinacridone magenta).

26 Remove the masking tape, then mix burnt sienna with Naples yellow for the main building on the left. Work carefully round the windows and detailing, and leave the paler areas white. Don't worry if you accidentally lose some of the whites.

27 Lay a creamy wash of Naples yellow with a little cerulean blue over the nearest building, up as far as the pillar tops of the white gothic arches. While it is still wet, change to the no. 3 brush and use a mid-grey mix of burnt sienna and cerulean blue to darken the shaded parts of the pillars. Keep one side of each pillar dark and one light, ready for them to be properly defined by the dark spaces between them later. Allow the paint to dry.

28 Wet the very dark areas within the building visible behind the façade and apply a dark mix of French ultramarine and burnt sienna, thus defining the pillars by infilling the dark spaces between them and leaving the pillars themselves alone. Put the shadow detailing on the pillar tops using the same colour. Lift out lighter patches within the shadows using paper towel.

29 Mix some burnt sienna, cerulean blue and a little quinacridone magenta for the top of the arched doorway, and put a little deep red into the shadows behind the pillars. Refer to the finished painting if necessary. Allow the paint to dry.

30 Mask out the wire mesh covering the arch and the windows either side using masking fluid applied with an Indian ink pen. Using a darker brown mix of burnt sienna, cerulean blue and a little Naples yellow, paint over the arch and take the colour down into the rest of the doorway. Use dry brushing to give texture. Add a line of colour for the detailing around the outside of the door. Using the very dark mix of French ultramarine and burnt sienna, put in the darkest darks within the doorway and lower windows. When the paint is dry, rub off the masking fluid from the mesh and from the flags.

31 Put in the base shadows on the flags using burnt sienna mixed with cerulean blue. Use the no. 3 brush. Allow them to dry, then paint the blue flag using cobalt blue, working roughly round the shapes of the stars. Apply the darker shadows using a mix of French ultramarine and burnt sienna. Paint the other flags using quinacridone magenta mixed with yellow ochre for the red, and phthalo green and yellow ochre for the green.

32 Paint the yellow stars on the blue flag using Naples yellow, then put in the quatrefoils on either side of the doorway arch. Moving to the next building along on the right, start to put in the windows, the canopy and some of the detailing, and build up the tones using burnt sienna, cerulean blue and yellow ochre. When dry, place the light windows with a light grey mix, and the dark windows with a mix of burnt sienna and Payne's gray. Strengthen the bottom of the buildings with a line of burnt sienna, with Payne's gray underneath it.

33 Block in the landing stage using burnt sienna mixed with a little cerulean blue, and add some Payne's gray to strengthen it, varying the tone a little with light and dark.

34 Re-wet the water using a large brush and mix a blue-green black using phthalo blue, burnt sienna and quinacridone magenta. This time put the colour in using broad, horizontal brushstrokes. Darken the area beneath the buildings in the background.

35 Smooth out the colour using a fan brush and allow to dry completely.

36 Use the same dark mix for the ripples under the buildings and landing stages to the left, then make a watery mix of phthalo blue and burnt sienna and put in the ripples on the foreground water. Use a no. 6 brush and work in random, horizontal strokes, using dry brushing here and there to add some texture. Use the same mix for the shadows under the distant jetty, and a dark of Payne's gray only for the foreground pole reflections.

Tip

Work quickly when painting water, to help suggest a sense of fluidity.

37 Look over the whole picture and put in the rest of the darks using Payne's gray, including the area under the nearby jetties. Darken the base of the buildings. Allow to dry thoroughly.

38 Rub off all the masking fluid, then put in the two red flagpoles on the second building from the left using burnt sienna mixed with quinacridone magenta. Use yellow ochre to define the distant boats and poles, and put in small touches of red on the buildings using a red of quinacridone magenta and cadmium lemon. Wet the poles and touch in blue-grey of cerulean blue and burnt sienna down their left sides. Apply the grey to the pale boat behind these poles. When dry, apply a grey stripe to the boat's side and darken its waterline.

39 When dry, use a small flat brush to put in the red stripes on the poles using quinacridone magenta and cadmium lemon. For the tops of the poles use cobalt turquoise light, straight from the tube, and Payne's gray for the black accents. Darken the base of the poles and drag up the colour from the water. Use burnt sienna for the wooden poles, then place cerulean blue down the shaded side and allow it to bleed across to the right.

40 Gently touch in the railings of the jetty with a little burnt sienna, leaving one or two white highlights. Allow to dry, then put in the black vertical cracks on the wooden poles in the foreground.

41 Carefully paint in the boat and gondolier with the tip of the brush using Payne's gray, leaving white highlights. Dot in the chimneys using yellow ochre mixed with a little quinacridone magenta, and put in any other missing details. Avoid overworking the details – keep them loose.

Tip

Cast your eye over your painting and compare it with the finished version. Make a list of what you still need to do, for example adding missing details, strengthening shadows or highlights, and straightening any lines.

The Heart of Venice

TRACING 5

I gained access to this viewpoint, with the Ponte Pignoli in front of me, one grey morning, from Calle de le Acque. The walkway through the pillars on the right is Sotoportego de le Acque.

We can decide not to paint some scenes because they seem too complicated. The solution is always in the drawing. Get a good drawing down, and you have a skeleton to flesh out. The initial washes here are very simple and, once in place, you simply work the rest of the painting in manageable portions. Focus on the small details one at a time, and the big picture will take care of itself. One of the secrets of painting Venice is to spot the red here and there. This gives it some intensity.

You will need

Paper: 55 x 36cm (21¾ x 14¼in), 300gsm (140lb) Arches rough watercolour paper

Colours: cadmium lemon, quinacridone gold, quinacridone red, cerulean blue, cobalt turquoise light, phthalo green, Naples yellow, yellow ochre, burnt sienna, light red, sepia, indigo, white gouache

Brushes: 2 sable rounds (nos 7 and 3), 1 large and 1 small flat brush, fan blender

Gum arabic

Colour shaper, Indian ink pen and masking fluid

1 Mask out the bridge, the poles, the lamps and the edges of the boats. Allow the masking fluid to dry completely.

2 Lay a toning wash of Naples yellow, cerulean blue and light red over all of the background, apart from the water and the sky. Use the large flat brush, changing to the smaller brush for the background buildings. Save some lights for windows.

3 Allow the paint to dry, then put more masking fluid on to the foliage on the left, the lines of the brickwork on the arch walls to the right and the wrought ironwork.

4 Using various mixes of Naples yellow, yellow ochre and light red, put in the brickwork on the right. Darken the tone above the brickwork slightly, then wet the sills and drop in a reddish-grey mix of cerulean blue, yellow ochre and light red.

5 Build up the colour under the sills using a grey-green mix of cerulean blue, burnt sienna and yellow ochre, then use a small flat brush to drag colour upwards to form the windows.

6 Continue putting the main darks on to the window sills, adding more cerulean blue to the mix to strengthen it where necessary. Use cerulean blue, burnt sienna and quinacridone gold to block in the door behind the balcony, dragging the paint upwards as before.

7 Use the edge of the small flat brush to put paint and texture on to the walls. Use different mixes of cerulean blue, yellow ochre and light red, and work with the natural beauty of the wash. As you come down, shift the mix slightly towards yellow. Avoid the light patches, and soften any hard edges as you work. Tilt the board slightly and allow the paint to dry naturally, allowing granulation to develop.

8 Continue across the building, then spatter on some water in some areas followed by a grey mix of cerulean blue and burnt sienna for the dark patches.

9 Continue to strengthen the colour on the front of the building, then start to put in the detailing and shadows using a black mix of sepia and indigo. Use the small flat brush for the surfaces and clean edges, and a no. 3 round for more detailed work. For the shadows under the stone ledge, wet the paper selectively and drag the darks down. Tilt the board as before to encourage granulation.

Tip

To help maintain vertical lines, paint along the edge of a straight piece of card.

10 Define the brickwork by locating the masked brickwork courses in your painting and referring to the finished image. Paint a very fine, horizontal line of Payne's grey just above most of the masked lines. Add some patches of strong light red to the brickwork. For the doorways, lay a very dark brown mix of sepia and indigo into the top part then drag the colour down, adding water as you go to lighten it and softening the bottom edge. Strengthen the right-hand side of the painting and add more detail and shadows. Use the tip of the flat brush and vertical strokes to accentuate the pillars. Wet above the nearby ledge to the right, leaving a gap along the ledge top. Add a mix of yellow ochre, cerulean blue and light red, leaving the ledge top light.

11 Continue to build up the colour on the pillars and add texture by dry brushing. Add some strong black marks here and there. Wet the surface of the ledge at the base of the buildings and put in an intense dark below it so that the colour bleeds up. For the lower right-hand part of the bridge, use a brown wash followed by the indigo and sepia mix for the strong darks.

12 Accentuate the black shadows within the building by dampening each area and dropping in indigo. Further define the coping stones forming the ledge at the base of the building, then rub off the masking fluid on the balcony and paint in the ironwork. Leave upward-facing facets light (refer to the finished painting).

13 Continue along to the right-hand buildings beyond the bridge, adding colour and detail using various mixes of cerulean blue, yellow ochre and light red. Start to build up the colour on the background buildings using similar mixes, but with Naples yellow instead of yellow ochre. First lay on a light wash then use the same colour to touch in the details. For window detail use a neutral grey mix of cerulean blue and burnt sienna.

14 Make a grey-green mix of cerulean blue, burnt sienna and yellow ochre and lay a light wash of colour over the left-hand buildings. Drop in some wet burnt sienna followed by cerulean blue then clean water to obtain a more interesting background. Tilt the board to blend the colours and achieve a granulated effect.

Tip

Work the painting in small phases and small, manageable areas, allowing each to dry.

15 Put in the background colour behind the foliage and build up additional layers of patterning on top of the masked-out leaves. Use a mix of burnt sienna, cerulean blue and light red, and bring in some yellow ochre towards the bottom of the picture. While still wet, introduce some rich darks using an indigo and light red mix, bringing the colour down from the top and working it in between the leaves. Allow the paint to dry.

16 Start to put in the darks and the detailing on the stone balustrade using a stronger version of the grey-green mix. Darken the shaded sides of the stone balusters and soften the leading edge. For the wooden balustrade use burnt sienna and for the metal railings behind it use dark grey. Fill in the darks and build up the layers beneath the balustrades using dark brown; for the deepest tones use indigo. Pull the darks down into the foliage.

17 Dry brush on the brickwork below the foliage using a strong red mix, then put in the dark openings and shadows using indigo – lay the colour on using the small flat brush then pull the paint up. Drag dark lines along the base of the walls.

Tip

Building transparent layers rather than one finished layer is often the key to successful watercolour.

18 Continue to build up rough, almost abstract, detailing on the left, mostly with straight verticals. Put in the iron gate at the side of the bridge, then remove the masking fluid from the section of bridge just below it, leaving the rest in place. Build up the darks behind the foliage and below the gate using a mix of cerulean blue and burnt sienna applied with the no. 7 brush. Put in another dark layer using indigo. For the detailing behind the foliage, change to the no. 3 round brush.

19 Darken the steps behind the gate using a brown-grey mix, then lay a shadow wash over each figure on the bridge using a mix of cerulean blue and burnt sienna. Leave a thin, white outline. Starting with the person on the left, add the man's head and a 'V' shape for the neck using light red, then add a little Naples yellow. Darken the brown hair, the neck and the jacket. Finally, darken the legs. Place a thin bar on the face for the eyes and a shadow under the nose.

20 Paint the other figures in the same way, using quinacridone red and cerulean blue for the woman's blouse. Position the clothes and the features carefully, and avoid overworking – it is more important to keep the shapes loose than to focus on the detail. Paint some vertical greys for the shapes between the pale balusters on the far side of the bridge.

21 Remove the masking fluid from the foliage on the left, then re-mask the lamps. Allow to dry, then with the no. 3 brush dab a mix of cadmium lemon, burnt sienna and phthalo green over the foliage, leaving a few small gaps. Allow to dry, then add a touch of indigo to the mix and dab on the darker green. Finally, after the second layer has dried, darken the mix further and weave a third layer of darks in amongst the first two. Tone down some of the lights if there are too many.

22 Cover up the rest of the painting with scrap paper and spatter some wet black-green paint over the foliage to create texture. Use the no. 7 brush. Allow to dry, then remove the masking fluid from the lamps and paint them using burnt sienna; for the tops and casing, mix the burnt sienna with cerulean blue to make a neutral grey. Leave the top right-hand facets on the lamps as light paper, and add the dark detail.

23 Add the detailing on the base of the left-hand building, then dampen the water and lay in a light wash of cerulean blue and burnt sienna using the no. 7 brush.

Tip

Before starting to paint the water, make sure you have plenty of colour mixed and that tubes of all the colours you need are readily to hand.

24 Allow to dry, then wet the area under the bridge and put in two or three vertical strokes of gum arabic using the no. 7 brush. Follow this with Naples yellow, light red, a grey mixed from cerulean blue and burnt sienna, phthalo green and cobalt turquoise mixed, and finally cobalt blue. Lay the colours in wet-into-wet vertical streaks, blending them a little.

25 Blend the colours together with a fan brush then revert to the no. 7 brush and put in the boat reflection in the water on the right. Use a mix of light red, Naples yellow, burnt sienna and cerulean blue and work in horizontal strokes. Re-wet the area under the bridge and start to lay in the phthalo green and cobalt turquoise. Keep it wet, but keep the boat reflection dry.

26 Gradually bring the colour down towards the bottom of the painting. Leave gaps where the lights are. Work with horizontal strokes. Keep the paint moving and re-wet if necessary to avoid it drying out.

27 Keeping it wet, lay an intense indigo under the bridge. Blend it in using the fan brush. Strengthen the dark reflections on the left-hand side and under the boat on the right. Mix the indigo with the phthalo green and cobalt turquoise to create a more muted version as you move down into the foreground.

28 Continue to build up the colour of the water, softening and blending it as you work. Put in the subtle reflections under the wall on the left using a mix of Naples yellow and light red. Now let it dry.

29 Remove the masking fluid from the red poles and the wooden posts next to the boat that is nearer the bridge, and wet the area under the steps on the right then darken it. Apply the colour in two layers, each time allowing the previous layer to dry and re-wetting before putting on the new wash of paint.

30 Wet the right-hand side of each red post and drop in a soft wash of grey down the right-hand sides only. When dry, brush in a strong quinacridone red, leaving the white tops and a few flecks of white in the red. Paint the small wooden posts with light red and cerulean blue, adding more blue to the right for shadow.

31 Start to paint the smaller of the two gondolas. Use light red, quinacridone red, grey (cerulean blue and burnt sienna) and a mix of Naples yellow and light red for the detail inside the boat.

32 Leave to dry, and use indigo to put in the dark shadows both inside and outside the boat. Leave a subtle highlight on the side of the boat, and stronger, white highlights here and there.

33 Put in the reds on the main gondola using quinacridone red, then map in the details using the same mixes as before, plus cerulean blue.

34 Lay in the greys in two layers – light first, then indigo. Work carefully around the detailing on the back of the boat. Build up the darks, leaving a subtle highlight on the side of the boat. Drag a little texture to the back of the chair.

35 Put in the red flowers on the left by dabbing colour into some of the lights. Allow to dry, then rub off all the remaining masking fluid. Put a variegated pale grey wash of cerulean blue, burnt sienna and yellow ochre over the bridge. Brush greys into the shadows on the balusters.

36 Intensify the shadows on the bridge using a darker grey, dry, then put in another, darker, layer. Define the detailing on the stonework using thin, dark lines, then dry brush a pale wash over the top to give texture. Lay an intense dark indigo underneath the bridge.

37 Strengthen the stone arch and the ledge on the right, then complete the brown pole using a plain wash of burnt sienna, wet on dry. Use indigo to put a shadow down the right-hand side of the pole, then intensify the indigo on the boat, painting over some of the whites to increase the effect of the rest.

38 Paint the railings at the side of the bridge using indigo, leaving a few white highlights. Put in the man's hands resting on the bridge, and add some subtle patches of red and turquoise to enliven the duller areas on the left.

39 Finally, intensify the dark shadows under the gondolas. Add soft highlights to the hull, wet on dry, using a white gouache, cerulean blue and Naples yellow mix. Blend with a fan blender or no. 7 round.

Tip

If you need more highlights on the boat, you can put these in with white gouache. Colours can be replaced by adding these to the white.

Rialto Bridge

TRACING
6

This early evening view was seen from the San Polo side of the south-west face of Rialto Bridge, near the Rialto market. The great arch is what catches your attention, but the skyline is of equal importance; it draws the top of the bridge and the buildings together. Masking this out allows one smooth, wet wash to be applied to the sky, which unifies the whole painting and gets you off to a good start. The yawning hole of an arch is easy to paint in comparison, but notice there is just enough light under it to sustain interest.

You will need

Paper: 55 x 36cm (21¾ x 14¼in), 300gsm (140lb) Arches rough watercolour paper

Colours: cadmium orange, quinacridone magenta, French ultramarine, cobalt blue, phthalo blue, cerulean blue, phthalo green, Naples yellow, yellow ochre, burnt sienna, Venetian red, Payne's gray

Brushes: 2 sable rounds (nos 6 and 3), 4cm (1½in) hake (or flat brush), small flat brush, fan brush

Colour shaper and masking fluid

Ruling pen and metal ruler

Masking tape

Paper towel

1 Mask out the tops of the buildings, then wet the sky and lay on a pale wash of yellow ochre and quinacridone magenta using a no. 6 round brush. This will give the sky density. Tilt the board back a little to prevent the pigment from gathering along the skyline. Apply a wash of cerulean blue and phthalo blue mixed, from the bottom of the sky upwards. You can do this with the sky wet from the previous wash, or dry it completely first and then re-wet it.

2 While it is still wet, add more cerulean blue to the mix and strengthen the colour of the sky, allow to dry, then use a mix of Venetian red and Payne's gray to put in the metalwork on the top of the buildings with a no. 3 brush. Allow this to dry, then rub off the masking fluid. Tip the board the other way to encourage pigment to flow from top to bottom. Revert to the no. 6 brush and lay a pale, watery, peach-brown wash of burnt sienna, quinacridone magenta and a little cerulean blue over the rest of the picture, working carefully around the gondola and the canal bank right of the bridge.

3 Use the no. 6 brush to lay a light wash of yellow ochre, cerulean blue and a little quinacridone magenta over the background buildings, starting at the side of the bridge. Change to the no. 3 brush for the more detailed sections, and work around the light tones on the top of the buildings.

4 Lay masking tape along the sides of the left-hand building, then apply masking fluid in straight lines across the façade using a ruling pen and a metal ruler. Also place masking fluid around the window arches and balconies. Allow to dry.

5 Lay an uneven wash of cerulean blue and yellow ochre over the building, starting with the dentil moulding at the top and working down, avoiding the windows.

6 Allow the paint to dry then rub off the masking fluid and remove the tape. Now mask out the window frames on the right-hand building – first the verticals, allowing the masking fluid to dry, then the horizontals. Lay on a wash of clean water, avoiding the windows, and then paint on a little cadmium orange using the no. 3 brush.

7 Use the small flat brush to lay Venetian red and go over the right-hand building. Use the no. 3 brush to go round the detailing. Put in the top of the left-hand building too using the same colour, first laying a strip of masking tape across the top of the moulding to obtain a straight edge. Remove the tape.

8 Mix Venetian red and yellow ochre and paint the red brickwork on the tower; make the tone lighter than that of the sky on the right and darker on the left. For the very top of the tower, use a blue-grey mix of cerulean blue and burnt sienna. Save some lights, then darken the shaded parts to obtain a three-dimensional effect.

9 Gradually build up the shadows over the tower in layers, starting with Venetian red mixed with blue-grey for the shadows on the brickwork, and finishing with Payne's gray for the very deepest shadows inside the tower.

10 Strengthen the shadows on the top of the left-hand building and on the right-hand buildings using the blue-grey mix. Put in the windows, altering the relative amounts of blue and brown in the mix to achieve the various colours.

11 Add a little orange to the blue-grey mix for the shutters and apply it using the small flat brush. For the dark red frames use Venetian red with a little Payne's gray; for the dark accents on the windows use Payne's gray. Paint the tall archway in the same way, and then the windows and shutters on the left-hand building. Add dots of Payne's gray for the spaces between the balusters on the balconies.

12 Put in the shadows and the windows under the dentil moulding at the top of the building, and the arched doorway at the bottom. Then paint the green canopy on the right-hand building using a mix of phthalo green and cadmium orange. For the café front below the canopy, use burnt sienna. Leave spaces for the detail to be added later. Lay a shadow across the lower right corner of the building using the blue-grey mix.

13 Put in the very dark accents with Payne's gray then, before it dries, add some lights to the shop front with Venetian red and yellow ochre to suggest activity. Lift out some of the colour from the tall archway to give it more form. Allow the paint to dry and rub the masking fluid from the window frames of the right-hand buildings.

14 Use masking fluid applied with a colour shaper to mask out the top of the balustrade, excluding the part that is in shadow; the ledges across the top of the shuttered doorways; and the inside of the boat (including the figures). Allow the masking fluid to dry, then tape over the top of the bridge as a ruling guide for painting the dentil moulding. Wet the shaded side of the painting using a 4cm (1½in) hake or flat brush.

15 Tilt the board towards the base to encourage granulation, then lay a mix of cerulean blue, burnt sienna and a little yellow ochre on to the shaded area using the no. 6 brush. Lighten the mix towards the right, and apply layers of colour to ensure the left is very dark. This will draw the viewer's attention into the middle of the painting. Smooth out the brushstrokes with a fan brush and soften any hard edges.

16 Allow to dry. Extend the masking tape back along the top of the building over the shaded area, and apply masking fluid to the rest of the balustrade. Paint in the dentil moulding below the taped roof area with the no. 3 brush, using the tape as a guide. Start with the lighter shadows, then place the darker ones in between. Start to apply detailing to the masonry on the bridge.

17 Make a dark green mix of cerulean blue and cadmium orange and paint in the shuttered doorways using the no. 3 brush.

18 The tape for the far-side bridge dentil moulding covered the central arch on the top of the bridge, so I pulled the tape back and defined the shade on the arch. While it is still wet, darken the shadows where needed using a stronger version of the same mix. Use a ruling pen and metal ruler to mask out the slats on the shutters (see step 4), and a colour shaper to add masking fluid to the people on the bridge.

19 Make a darker green using cerulean blue, burnt sienna and phthalo green and paint in the slats and detailing on the shuttered doorways. For the extreme darks, use Payne's gray. Lift some vertical strips of colour with a damp brush, dab with paper towel, and paint in some streaks and patches of burnt sienna.

20 Use the tip of the no. 3 brush to put in the detailing on the central arch and the dentil moulding detail on the top of the bridge on the right using the masking tape as a stencil. Use a mix of burnt sienna, yellow ochre and cerulean blue. Deepen, then apply the hard-edged shadow within the arch. Remove the masking tape and place a fine line above the dentil moulding. When dry, rub off the masking fluid.

21 Use the burnt sienna, yellow ochre and cerulean blue mix to apply grey detailing on the bridge balustrade with lines and marks. Refer to the finished painting.

22 While the paint is drying, lay a strip of masking tape along the top of the dentil moulding below the balustrade on the left, and put in the shadows between the bricks using a strong version of the cerulean blue, burnt sienna and yellow ochre mix.

23 Allow to dry, then move the masking tape to align with the base of the balustrade. Dampen each baluster in turn and add Payne's gray around the base and the left-hand side, allowing the colour to bleed upwards. Also darken the shadows elsewhere on the balustrade. When dry, use the very dark green mix to paint in the spaces in between the balusters.

24 Remove the masking tape and strengthen the shadow underneath the balustrade – dampen it first using the no. 6 brush, then add cerulean blue and burnt sienna; for the darkest shadows add a touch of Payne's gray over the top.

25 Continue to strengthen the shadows along and below the balustrade, and add definition to the stonework by outlining individual bricks and stones using the tip of the no. 3 brush. Make the detailing less pronounced as you move towards the right of the picture.

26 Take the detailing down into the main part of the bridge and use dry brushing to trace around the stonework using a dark grey mix of cerulean blue and burnt sienna. Strengthen the lines in places to obtain an uneven finish. Observe the directions of the lines carefully to obtain a realistic perspective.

27 Define the brickwork and shadows around the arch of the bridge, thickening the lines as you come down towards the base on the left. Using a dry, small flat brush, drag water down over the stone plaque to lift out colour and create texture. Use the tip of the brush to outline the plaque.

28 Using a very wet, dark mix of cerulean blue and burnt sienna, put in the steps on the left using the no. 6 brush. Allow to dry, and add the darkest tones using an intense mix of French ultramarine and Venetian red.

29 Mask out the lighter stone at the base of the arch, then wet the left-hand side of the bridge and lay in some burnt sienna and a touch of Payne's gray in vertical, upwards brushstrokes to mimic the staining caused by damp.

30 Blend in a little cerulean blue and burnt sienna mix, and apply some smaller rust patches of burnt sienna and yellow ochre towards the centre of the bridge. Drag the colour down and blend it in as before. Use a smaller brush if necessary.

31 Continue with the detailing on the right of the picture, allow to dry, then strengthen with the cerulean blue and burnt sienna mix, using Payne's gray for the deepest darks. Put in the base colour for the street on the right using a light wash of burnt sienna.

32 Put in the shuttered doorways that are just visible on the right-hand side of the bridge using the same green as you used before (see steps 17–19). Remove masking fluid from the people on the bridge then start to paint them. First mask out the balustrade then put in the heads using Venetian red and Naples yellow. Add the clothes using various yellows, greens, reds, oranges and greys.

33 Remove the masking tape and put in some reds for the people on the far side of the canal. Use a ruling pen to mask out the legs of the tables and chairs, allow it to dry and lay a light wash of burnt sienna over the top, leaving some light areas. Put in the heads and some of the bodies of the people in the crowd using the same colour.

34 Make a dark mix of cerulean blue and burnt sienna, and put in the bulk of the people. Where the tables and chairs touch the ground, add randomly placed horizontal lines to indicate the shadows.

35 Add the more intense darks using a stronger version of the same mix, then use yellow ochre and Venetian red for the people on the far right end of the bridge. Strengthen the edge of the canal using burnt sienna.

36 Mask out the lighter-coloured stonework around the arch of the bridge using a colour shaper and allow it to dry. Using the no. 6 brush, drop in some yellow ochre, working wet on dry, under the arch, followed by some burnt sienna.

37 Add some French ultramarine at the top of the arch and drag it down, following the curve of the bridge. Build up the colour, and introduce some horizontal brushstrokes at the base of the arch to indicate form.

38 Continue to build up the dark blues using strong vertical and horizontal brushstrokes, then change to the no. 3 brush and drag some rust in the form of burnt sienna up from the base of the bridge. Define the bottom edge and the back of the bridge by putting in a very strong line of French ultramarine, bleeding it upwards in places.

39 Mask out the highlights on the end of the boat and the oar, then make a very wet mix of Naples yellow and cadmium orange and lay it over the water, including the boat if you wish. Use the no. 6 brush. Make the mix slightly stronger on the left of the painting.

40 While the paint is still wet, lay in some Venetian red on the right, followed by phthalo blue mixed with phthalo green for darks in the water. Take this latter colour down next to the red and under the bridge, adding in more blue to the mix in the foreground.

41 Continue building up the darks using strong brushstrokes to achieve a variegated effect. Leave a thin yellow line along the base of the bridge, and add in a little Payne's gray where the face of the bridge would be reflected. Blend the colours together by brushing downwards with a fan blender.

42 Darken the water on the right a little, leaving a strong suggestion of red for the reflected buildings, then allow the paint to dry. Lift out some horizontal lights behind the boat by first wetting with a damp brush then dabbing off with paper towel. Touch some colour back in using yellow ochre.

43 Use a mix of Payne's gray and phthalo blue to paint over the gondola. With the same mix, add some more dark to the far right-hand side of the street. Allow to dry.

> **Tip**
>
> Working out where to leave whites is a challenge. Refer to the finished painting and copy the pattern of lights closely. It is better to leave too many lights than too few.

44 With Venetian red, put in the gondolier's head, then add some black to the head using the dark mix of Payne's gray and phthalo blue. Continue with this mix for his body. Dry thoroughly, then rub off the masking fluid. Dot in the heads of the people in the boat using Venetian red, then touch in the features.

45 Complete the people in the boat using red, blue and black, leaving some whites here and there. Deepen the colour of the boat if necessary, and place some pale phthalo blue in some of the highlights around the stern of the boat, and Naples yellow on the ferro at the bow.

46 Starting with the no. 6 brush, build up the reflections of the ripples under the boat using a mix of phthalo green, phthalo blue and Payne's gray. Use dry brushing, and work from the boat downwards. Change to the no. 3 brush for the finer reflections.

47 Put in the black railings in the lower left part of the picture using the tip of the no. 3 brush, then dab in the red flowers using a mix of Venetian red and quinacridone magenta. Use the same red to enliven some of the darks here and there. Remove the masking fluid from the arch of the bridge and darken it slightly with a little cerulean blue and burnt sienna. Use dry brushing to bring out the texture in places.

Index

Palazzo Ducale

41.5 x 29cm (16½ x 11½in)

The Palazzo Ducale (Doge's Palace) has a subtle hue which looks yellow but is actually pale grey/orange. Observe what colours really are before you interpret them. I wanted a dark sky to contrast with the building. Several layers of red, yellow, orange and blue applied wet in wet, one after another, gave a dense sky tone and an undercoat for the water. Once dry, the rest of the painting was worked one piece at a time, concentrating on the basic proportions. The Venetian Gothic architecture consists of endless repetitive detail, so I didn't worry about achieving extreme accuracy. Instead, I introduced some variation, which added interest.

For the water, with two coats in place I used the natural shape of the brush to drag wet, flowing colour across in long, rippling, wavy shapes. The foreground ripples are larger, and many of the ripples join together to create another set of negative shapes in between them. Finally, I painted the gondolas with their figures, which were masked out at the outset.